Making a Difference:

Putting Jewish Spirituality Into Action, One Mitzvah at a Time

Bradley Shavit Artson and **Gila Gevirtz**

Educational and Developmental Consultants
Paula Mack Drill, M.S.W.
David Yammer, Ph.D.

Project Manager: **Gila Gevirtz**

Designer: **Pronto Design and Production, Inc.**

The authors and publisher gratefully acknowledge the following sources of photographs and graphic images for this book:

Bill Aron 23 (top right), 76 (top), 137 (left); **Kathy Bloomfield** 12 (right), 20, 21 (top left and bottom right), 93 (right), 97; **Consulate General of Israel in New York** 37; **Creative Image Photography** 12 (left), 13, 17, 24 (top), 31, 40 (top center and top right), 43 (center left and top right), 44 (bottom), 55, 57 (top), 69 (top), 84 (bottom), 94 (bottom), 101, 102 (top), 106-7, 108 (left), 109, 113 (top), 119 (top center), 122, 125 (right), 130 (left of middle), 132, 135; **Gustav Doré** 21 (top right), 50, 112; **Eileen Elterman** 71 (top), 74; **Gila Gevirtz** 15, 36 (bottom), 52, 60, 61, 64-65, 72, 79, 85 (right), 92, 111 (top left), 114, 131; **Steve Goodman** 44 (top); **David Hollander/Congregation B'nai Jeshurun, Short Hills, NJ** 136; **International Ladies Garment Workers Union Archives** 18; **Israeli Scouts** 57 (bottom); **Israel Ministry of Tourism** 40 (right and bottom), 48 (bottom), 56 (top), 81, 108 (right); **Jewish Theological Seminary, Joseph and Miriam Ratner Center for the Study of Conservative Judaism** 36 (top); **Francene Keery** 71 (bottom), 76 (bottom), 127 (top); **L. Lowenthal** 78 (top center and top right); **Kurt Meyerowitz** 86 (bottom); **NASA** cover (top), 63; **New Jersey Newsphotos** 115 (left); **New York Public Library** 19; **Ilene Perlman** 58; **Hara Person** 23 (bottom right), 83; **Sheila Plotkin** 137 (right); **H. Roger-Viollet** 71 (middle); **April Saul** 90 (right); **Clare Sieffert** cover (bottom left and bottom right), 11, 45, 82, 120; **SuperStock** 7, 9, 28, 32, 86, 89, 111 (bottom), 125 (left), 139; **Union of American Hebrew Congregations** 78 (top left, middle center, and bottom right), 119 (top left), 126 (left); **Therese Wagner** 22; **Michael Wasserman** 24 (bottom); **Sunny Yellen** 68, 100, 121; **Alan Zale/New York Times Pictures** 10; **Zionist Archives and Library** 53.

Published by Behrman House, Inc.
Springfield, NJ 07081
www.behrmanhouse.com

Library of Congress Cataloging-in-Publication Data

Artson, Bradley Shavit.
    Making a difference : putting Jewish spirituality into action, one mitzvah at a time / by
Bradley Shavit Artson and Gila Gevirtz.
        p. cm.
    ISBN 0-87441-712-0
        1. Jewish teenagers—Conduct of life—Juvenile literature. 2. Jewish way of
life—Juvenile literature. 3. Ethics, Jewish—Juvenile literature. 4. Jewish religious
education—Textbooks for teenagers. [1. Teenagers. 2. Jewish way of life. 3. Ethics,
Jewish. 4. Jewish religious education. 5. Conduct of life.] I. Gevirtz, Gila. II. Title.

BM727 .A78 2001
296.7'0835—dc21

                                                                                            2001016140

Manufactured in the United States of America

To Shira and Jacob, Benjamin, and Sydney

"The Holy Blessing One gave the Torah in the month of Sivan because the sign of Sivan is Twins, and the Twins are human, and being human they have mouths to speak together, and hands to clap together, and feet to dance together" (Pesiḥta Rabbati, Piska 20).

May you speak together in love and wisdom, clap together in shared joy, and dance your whole lives long.
—BSA

And to the West End Synagogue community

For your friendship and generosity, your encouragement and wisdom, I thank you.
—GG

Table of Contents

① Getting Connected

What will my life be like when I'm an adult? What will I look like? Where will I live? Will I be famous? happy? loved?

So many questions. We all have dreams about how we want our lives to be. If only we could know whether or not our dreams will come true. If only there were a time machine to hop on, or virtual reality software to project the future. But there is no such machine or software, and becoming an adult takes a long time.

So what can we do? We can't know the future. No matter how impatient we are, there's no way to predict it. But even so, we can help our dreams come true. We can take actions *now* that will make a difference *later*. There's even a plan, a roadmap we inherited, that will help us become adults we can be proud of being, adults who will make our dreams come true. This roadmap is the treasure of the Torah and its tradition of mitzvot.

Perhaps you think this can't be so. Perhaps you think mitzvot are actions you take to help or to please someone else, not to improve your own life. That's understandable—so many mitzvot do help other people or bring pleasure to others by providing them with food, shelter, medicine, clothing, and companionship. But when you perform a mitzvah, you don't just help someone else or observe an ancient custom, you also create a link between yourself and God.

The Torah teaches that God made a sacred agreement—called the *Brit,* or Covenant—with the Jewish people. Through the *Brit,* God promised to make us a holy nation if we promised to fulfill the mitzvot. In Hebrew, *mitzvot* means "commandments." But in Aramaic, another ancient Jewish language, *mitzvot* means "connections." Each time we perform a mitzvah, we affirm the Covenant and our sacred connection to God.

The holiness of the mitzvot you perform, such as bringing comfort to someone who is ill or lighting Shabbat and holiday candles, rubs off on you, filling in the details of who you are. Each mitzvah is like a brushstroke of a sacred hue—the color of compassion, joy, generosity, respect, and honesty. Slowly, over time, the portrait of the adult you emerges, richer and more complex than a work of art.

Bar or Bat Mitzvah for a Day or for a Lifetime?

Preparing to become a bar or bat mitzvah—pouring over the roadmap and studying its many twists and turns—takes years. But for some young people, *being* a bar or bat mitzvah is a one-day affair. They work hard to prepare for the celebration—learning to read Hebrew, studying the Bible, practicing the synagogue service, and writing a *d'var Torah,* or speech. On the day of the celebration, they dress up in suits or dresses, and walk taller and with more dignity than ever before. However, when the last good-bye is said and they change back into their shorts or jeans, it seems as if everything is over, except for the task of writing thank-you notes and the pleasure of a few trinkets and games. For such teens, all the preparation was just for this one day, rather than for something bigger, more powerful, more important.

Living as a bat or bar mitzvah for only a day is much like learning how to ride a bike or how to play a guitar, then stopping just when you get good at it—just when you can travel a distance or make beautiful music. What was the point of all the effort? How will you or anyone else benefit from the skills you worked so hard to develop?

Sure, the celebration feels wonderful (once you finish your speech and return to your seat!), but your training and hard work are meant to help you enjoy more than that one day. Just as bicycling strengthens your heart, lungs, and leg muscles; just as playing the guitar builds the muscles in your arms and fingers, and your sensitivity to sound and music—so, too, by *living* as a bat or bar mitzvah you develop your character, your values, your self-confidence, and your spirit. You build your relationship with God, your friendships within the community, and your ability to express yourself through Jewish rituals and traditions.

Extraordinary vs. Superhuman

The holiness of living as a bar or bat mitzvah can transform ordinary days into extraordinary days. It can even transform an ordinary person into an extraordinary person.

Making a Difference will show you how being a bat or bar mitzvah can last a lifetime and produce a lifetime of meaning and joy. It will teach you that you don't have to be superhuman to be extraordinary. And it will help you learn to live as an adult Jew by performing one mitzvah at a time—perhaps never perfectly, certainly never in a superhuman way, but always to the best of your ability, always improving, strengthening, and enriching the person you are.

② Taking Action

Choose life...by loving Adonai your God, heeding God's mitzvot, and holding fast to God. For thereby you shall have life.

—Deuteronomy 30:19–20

Jewish tradition teaches that God's presence can be found in the wonders of daily life—the arc of a jump shot that falls smoothly through the basketball hoop, the sight of the setting sun melting into a shimmering pool of purple-red light, and the scent of freshly mowed grass in early spring. Our tradition also teaches that it is our partnership with God—the *Brit*, or Covenant—that helps transform what would otherwise be ordinary lives into extraordinary lives.

The Ten Commandments

1. I am Adonai your God who brought you out of Egypt.

2. Do not have other gods beside Me or pray to idols.

3. Do not use My name except for holy purposes.

4. Remember Shabbat and keep it holy.

5. Honor your father and mother.

6. Do not murder.

7. Do not commit adultery.

8. Do not steal.

9. Do not swear falsely.

10. Do not desire what belongs to your neighbor.

 think about it!

WHAT WOULD IT MEAN TO LIVE AS JEWS IF WE HAD NOT RECEIVED THE MITZVOT?

◄ Our tradition teaches that each of us is obligated to study the Torah throughout our lives. This is Judith Kaplan Eisenstein. In 1922, she became the first girl ever to celebrate her bat mitzvah with a ceremony in the synagogue. She is shown here at the 70th anniversary of her bat mitzvah celebration.

We Received the Torah at Mount Sinai

The Torah teaches that after entering into the *Brit* with the Israelites, God told Moses that the people were ready to receive the mitzvot. God spoke, and the Israelites received the Ten Commandments.

After the Ten Commandments were given, our tradition teaches, Moses received the other laws of Torah from God (making a total of 613 commandments). Moses taught the mitzvot to the children of Israel so we could become a holy people, an *am kadosh*.

Our Prophets and Sages

In every generation, we continue to study the Torah. We also study other sacred texts, such as the books of the prophets and the teachings of our ancient sages, the rabbis, to learn how we can become our best selves, serve God, and add holiness to the world.

From the prophets Isaiah, Zechariah, and Hosea we learn that our observance of holy days and rituals are important, but that fulfilling these mitzvot pleases God only if we also observe the mitzvot of treating one another with respect, kindness, and justice. And from Elijah we learn that although God did not *create* Jews differently from others, there are times when we must *behave* differently if we are to live as a holy people. For example, though the laws of many countries make it illegal to be cruel to animals, they do not require people to help animals in need. In contrast, Jewish law, or *halachah*, requires us to be compassionate to animals. We are commanded to provide cold and hungry animals with food and shelter, and to feed pets before we feed ourselves.

▲ A special cup is set at the Passover seder for Elijah, the prophet who, tradition teaches, will herald the coming of the Messiah—an age of universal peace, prosperity, and justice. But even as we pray that the Messiah will come quickly, we live in the here and now by working to improve the world.

Ritual and Ethical Mitzvot

Unique among the teachings of ancient peoples (and still rare to this day), the Torah insists that a combination of ritual and ethical mitzvot is necessary for living as a holy people. Therefore, we perform ritual mitzvot, such as praying, eating matzah on Passover, and reading the megillah on Purim, as well as ethical mitzvot, such as providing those in need with food, clothing, and the opportunity to work or study.

The ancient rabbis wrote the Talmud to help us understand how to perform mitzvot. For example, the Torah instructs us to celebrate Sukkot by "living in booths for seven days." But it was the rabbis who explained how to build a sukkah: what materials to use, how high to make the walls, and what to use for the roof. The sages taught us how the mitzvot should guide our behavior—how they can help us raise children, run businesses, build communities, spend our leisure time, and celebrate holy days.

The teachings of modern sages help us understand how we can perform mitzvot in our own time. For even today, and perhaps *especially* today, amid the hubbub of Web sites, cloning, space travel, and constant change, mitzvot can continue to make us more loving and kinder people by helping us bring peace, beauty, justice, compassion, and holiness into the world.

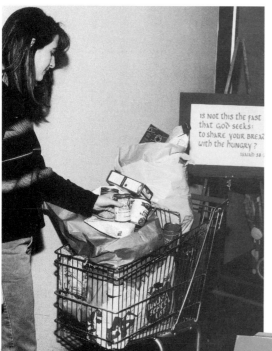

◀ **Many synagogues conduct High Holy Day food drives, reminding us of the importance of both praying and feeding the hungry.**

▶ **Appreciating the caring acts of others—the times people offer us help or a hug—can remind us of our own ability to make a difference in people's lives. What act of kindness did you perform today?**

WHAT WAS THE KINDEST THING ANYBODY DID FOR YOU TODAY?

The Choices You Make Are Important

Our sages taught that we are the authors of our own lives. Every day, the choices we make fill another page with our stories. These can be wonderful stories of hard work and celebration, love and kindness, honesty and fairness.

By studying, working, praying, and celebrating with the Jewish community, we can help each other make good choices. When we study Torah together, we are reminded to honor the Covenant by observing mitzvot. When we work together on *bikkur ḥolim* and tzedakah projects, such as visiting the sick and clothing the poor, we share the rewards of living compassionate lives. And when we pray and celebrate together, we help create a loving community for ourselves and for others.

As you read *Making a Difference,* you will have many opportunities to think about these possibilities and how they relate to the person you are and the person you are becoming. You will be asked to consider the choices you make now and those you will make in the future. And you will be called upon to live a life of action, a life that transforms the sacred words of Torah into holy deeds.

◄ Jewish tradition teaches that the stories, dreams, and prayers of our people belong to the entire community.

Teens
Make a Difference
Mark Guterman

Mark Guterman knows how to work with and inspire others to make a difference in the world. The seeds of Operation Sports Stuff, a national community service run by teenagers, were sown when Mark set out to do his bar mitzvah project. Mark recycled "gently used" sports equipment—basketballs, baseballs and bats, soccer cleats, bicycles, tennis racquets, and lacrosse and hockey sticks—by collecting them from friends and neighbors in his Millburn, New Jersey community and donating them to poor children.

Impressed by Mark's creativity and initiative, *Sports Illustrated for Kids* ran a story about the project. The result: Mark received hundreds of calls from teens asking how they could develop similar projects. In response, he created an information packet outlining the how-tos of his project. By June 2000, there were 540 Operation Sports Stuff projects around North America. Teens in 16 states now coordinate these efforts, and more than half a million pieces of used equipment have been donated and distributed to the needy—proving once again that teens have the power, smarts, talent, and determination to make important choices and to make a difference!

Mark explains how it all started. "The inspiration for this project came from my father, Joel, who died of cancer two years ago. He was the chairman of our temple's 'Giving' group and he always organized blanket and clothing drives for homeless shelters. My project is a tribute to his generosity and an honor to his memory." ☼

What You Choose Is Telling

The choices we make affect how we see ourselves as well as how others see us. For example, people who choose to eat healthfully are seen as having self-discipline and high self-esteem, while those who never stray from a strict regimen are seen as inflexible.

Describe a choice you have made that reveals something about how you see yourself. What may it tell others about you and what you value?

_____

_____

_____

_____

_____

▼ **Mark Guterman (left), gets help from his friends, Daniel Spicehandler (center) and Michael Kimmel.**

Self-Portrait

★ WHEN I NEED TO MAKE DIFFICULT CHOICES OR IMPORTANT DECISIONS, I: (CHECK AS MANY RESPONSES AS ARE APPROPRIATE)

_____ LIST THE PROS AND CONS OF EACH OPTION

_____ DISCUSS IT WITH MY PARENTS

_____ OBSESS ABOUT IT

_____ TRY NOT TO THINK ABOUT IT

_____ LOG ONTO A CHAT ROOM

_____ PRAY

_____ PHONE OR E-MAIL FRIENDS

_____ HOLE UP IN MY ROOM

_____ GET AN UPSET STOMACH

_____ LISTEN TO MUSIC

OTHER: _____

YOU DON'T SAY!

"OPPORTUNITY MAY KNOCK ONLY ONCE, BUT TEMPTATION LEANS ON THE DOORBELL."
—*Author unknown*

WHAT HELPS YOU MAKE GOOD CHOICES WHEN "TEMPTATION LEANS ON THE DOORBELL"?

_____

_____

_____

▲ Life is more complicated than car repair. None of us can guarantee that our efforts to improve the world will always work out the way we want. But if each of us does our part, we can certainly make a difference.

think about it!

THE ANCIENT SAGE RABBI TARFON TAUGHT THAT NONE OF US IS RESPONSIBLE FOR MAKING THE WORLD PERFECT, BUT ALL OF US ARE RESPONSIBLE FOR DOING OUR PART TO IMPROVE THE WORLD. ARE YOU A PERSON WHO SOMETIMES TAKES RESPONSIBILITY FOR MORE THAN YOU NEED TO? WHEN? ARE YOU A PERSON WHO SOMETIMES AVOIDS RESPONSIBILITY? WHEN?

The **Book** of Your Life

EACH TIME YOU MAKE A CHOICE ABOUT HOW TO TREAT YOURSELF AND OTHERS, YOUR DECISION LEADS TO ANOTHER STORY IN YOUR "BOOK OF LIFE." WHAT ARE SOME OF YOUR STORIES? WHAT GOOD CHOICES HAVE YOU MADE EVEN WHEN DOING SO WAS DIFFICULT? WERE YOU ABLE TO SPEAK THE TRUTH AT A MOMENT WHEN IT WAS TEMPTING TO LIE? WERE YOU WILLING TO TAKE THE TIME TO HELP OTHERS EVEN WHEN IT WOULD HAVE BEEN EASIER TO IGNORE THEM?

DESCRIBE A GOOD BUT DIFFICULT CHOICE YOU MADE. WHAT HELPED OR INSPIRED YOU TO MAKE THAT CHOICE?

_____

_____

_____

_____

_____

THINK OF A CHOICE YOU MADE THAT YOU NOW REGRET. WHAT DID YOU LEARN FROM THAT EXPERIENCE?

_____

_____

_____

THINK ABOUT A GOAL YOU HAVE. WHAT CHOICES MUST YOU MAKE SO THAT IT BECOMES A STORY THAT ENRICHES YOUR BOOK OF LIFE?

_____

_____

_____

_____

_____

_____

③ Tzedakah

giving justly

[One] should be more concerned with spiritual than with material matters, but another person's material welfare is [one's] spiritual concern.

—Rabbi Israel Salanter

At one time or another, *everyone* gives charity. But some people *never* give tzedakah.

We are all taught to share with people who do not have as much as we do. Young children are asked to give a dime or a dollar to help clothe the poor and feed the hungry. Many teens participate in walkathons, bikathons, telethons, phonathons, and raffles to raise money for medical research, school programs, flood relief, and animal shelters. Some philanthropists donate millions of dollars, almost single-handedly funding orphanages, community centers, schools, and hospitals. But all these contributions, no matter how generous or important, may only be charity, and charity just isn't enough.

Charity vs. Tzedakah

Charity comes from the Latin word *caritas*, meaning "from the heart." And so it is. Charity is given from the heart, voluntarily, when and if and how much we feel like giving—no strings attached. That's good on the days we feel generous. But what happens when we feel stingy? indifferent? distracted? self-centered? What are the hungry, the homeless, and the ill to do then? What is to keep them going until the next time we are in the mood to give?

Tzedakah.

Recognizing that our emotions can be unpredictable, Jewish tradition does not rely on our kind impulses alone to make sure that the needs of the hungry, the homeless, and the ill are met. Instead it obligates us to perform acts of tzedakah—the giving of our time, our talent, or our money—no matter how we feel. Generous or stingy, caring or indifferent, we must give tzedakah frequently and with an open hand—whatever our age, ability level, or financial circumstances.

▲ In 1909, Clara Lemlich (shown on stage with her hand raised) was a teenage garment worker and activist who stood up for *tzedek*, justice, for herself and for others. In response to intolerable working conditions in New York's sweatshops, she called for a strike. Inspired by Clara's courage, thousands raised their hands in support. The strike became known as the Uprising of the Twenty Thousand.

▲ This 18th-century French Purim dish is decorated with words from Megillat Esther. It includes a portion of chapter 9, verse 22, which speaks of celebrating Purim by both feasting and giving gifts to the poor.

Reach Out and Help Someone

Just as Judaism teaches us to live each day with gratitude for the good in our lives, so it also asks us to continually add goodness to the lives of others. That is why many Jews celebrate life-cycle events, such as baby namings and weddings, not just with gifts and prayers of thanks, but also with donations to hospitals and medical research facilities. That is why we observe holidays such as Rosh Hashanah and Purim not only by reading from sacred texts and eating special foods—for example, honey-cake and hamantashen—but also by collecting food for the poor or volunteering in soup kitchens. And that is why on any day, even the most ordinary—perhaps, *particularly* on the most ordinary—we recite blessings of praise *and* reach out to help those in need.

When we give tzedakah we remind ourselves that we have been given much and that we have much to give. We are reassured that Jewish tradition will always help us become the best people we can be, no matter what our mood.

Did You Know?

IN THE UNITED STATES, THE POOREST PEOPLE GIVE A LARGER PERCENTAGE OF THEIR INCOMES TO CHARITY THAN DO THE WEALTHY. DOES THIS SURPRISE YOU? WHY OR WHY NOT?

_____

_____

Levels of Tzedakah

Moses Maimonides (1135–1204), also known as the Rambam, was a great rabbi, author, philosopher, physician, and community leader. He defined eight levels of tzedakah, moving from the least to the most praiseworthy. The levels are listed below, out of sequence. In the blank spaces, number the levels from 1 to 8 to show where you think each is in the sequence. The least praiseworthy level should be numbered "1" and the most praiseworthy "8." The Rambam's order appears upside down at the end of the list.

___ A. Giving before being asked

___ B. Giving graciously, but less than one should

___ C. Giving anonymously

___ D. Giving without knowing the identity of the recipient, although the recipient knows the identity of the donor

___ E. Giving reluctantly and with regret

___ F. Giving what one should, but only after being asked

___ G. Helping the recipient become self-supporting through a gift or a loan, or by finding employment for the recipient

___ H. Giving without knowing the identity of the recipient, and without the recipient knowing the identity of the donor

Do you agree or disagree with the Rambam's sequence? Why?

_____

_____

_____

Why do you think the eighth level is considered the highest?

_____

_____

The Rambam's sequence is 1 (E); 2 (B); 3 (F); 4 (A); 5 (D); 6 (C); 7 (H); 8 (G).

Creating A Balance

Tzedakah is a form of self-taxation. As Jews, we are obligated to donate at least 10 percent of our annual earnings to tzedakah. But, according to the ancient rabbis, we must contribute no more than 20 percent of our earnings: If we give away too much, we risk becoming poor ourselves.

The key to making the world a more just place is to create a balance between caring for ourselves and showing concern for others. The ancient sage Hillel taught: "If I am not for myself, who is for me? If I am only for myself, what am I? And if not now, when?"

List two ways you apply Hillel's philosophy to your own life by (1) doing something for yourself and (2) helping others.

_____

_____

Why do you think Hillel added, "And if not now, when?"

_____

_____

At the end of the Avon three-day walkathon for breast cancer, participants were exhausted but proud that they could make a difference by raising money for medical research.

How Should Tzedakah Be Given?

Jewish tradition not only requires us to give to the less fortunate, it also demands that we preserve their dignity. In biblical times, farmers followed the Torah's instruction to leave the harvest of the corners of the fields for the poor so that they would not have to beg.

Today, we continue to observe these teachings by setting aside a portion of our income to contribute to those in need. As a student you may have limited money to donate. But you do have a "field" of time, talents, and skills, some of which you can dedicate to making the world a better place.

Describe two ways in which people volunteering in a soup kitchen can help preserve the dignity of those they serve. (*Hint:* How does a host show respect to a guest?)

_____

_____

_____

List five programs that accept volunteers your age—do some research if necessary—and rank them from 1 to 5, going from the one you most want to participate in to the one you least want to participate in. Explain what makes number 1 of such interest to you.

_____

_____

_____

_____

_____

▲ The Bible tells how our ancestor Ruth gathered sheaves of grain that were left for the poor: "And she gleaned in the field after the reapers" (Ruth 2:3).

"HUMAN BEINGS ARE GOD'S LANGUAGE."
—*Hasidic saying*

WHAT DO YOU THINK THIS SAYING MEANS?

_____

_____

_____

The Jewish tradition of tzedakah, of caring for others, has always connected Jews to one another and to the rest of humanity. Here are a few ways to strengthen that connection by making tzedakah a regular part of your life.

Ready! Set! Go!

 **Place a tzedakah box in a central and convenient place in your home, perhaps on a kitchen counter.** During the week have members of your family put loose change in the box. On Friday evening, right before you light the Shabbat candles, add an additional amount of tzedakah.

Once or twice a year—for example, during the days between Rosh Hashanah and Yom Kippur, or just before Passover—gather the family together to decide how to distribute the tzedakah. For instance, you may want to give a portion of the money to an organization that you are a member of, such as your synagogue; a portion to a Jewish organization that serves the larger community, such as your local Jewish federation; and a portion to another community organization, such as a hospital, a soup kitchen, or a local animal shelter.

After a simhah—a joyous event—donate the flowers and left-over food to a community organization.

Work with your synagogue to help congregants who have simhas, such as weddings, bar or bat mitzvah celebrations, and baby namings, make arrangements with such institutions. Soup kitchens and shelters will be able to use the food, while hospitals and nursing homes may appreciate the good cheer of fresh flowers. Consider personally delivering the items with your family or friends.

▲ A simhah is a beautiful and sacred affair. Acts of tzedakah add to its beauty and holiness.

Participate in a tzedakah project with friends or family. In the spirit of a holiday, such as Tu B'Shevat or Thanksgiving, or as part of a birthday celebration, volunteer at a community agency. For example, you might help clean up a beach or park, plant or weed a flower bed at your synagogue, serve a Shabbat meal at a nursing home, or play board games and teach arts and crafts to children in a hospital. Here's another idea—most Jewish federations have an annual "Super Sunday" phonathon for which they recruit volunteers. Try it. There's a good chance you'll like it!

4 **Organize a fund-raising project for your religious school or synagogue.** Our tradition stresses the importance of working together as a community. So, get together with your classmates to identify a need that cannot be met by one person alone. Perhaps the library needs a computer, or maybe you want to build a collection of Jewish CDs and videos. You might plan a raffle, asking local businesses to contribute prizes, or you might organize a used-book sale, a magic show, or a talent night to which you can invite friends, family, and other congregants.

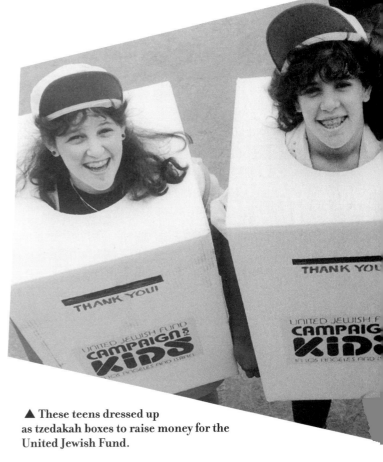

▲ These teens dressed up as tzedakah boxes to raise money for the United Jewish Fund.

▼ Try to organize tzedakah projects that will be interesting and fun to work on, for example, a carnival to raise scholarship money for a teen summer program in Israel.

5 **Search your home for useful items that you or your family no longer need.** Collect toys, sports equipment, clothes, blankets, books, appliances, furniture, and kitchen utensils that are clean and in good condition. Contact your local Jewish federation or other community agencies that can distribute such items to families in need.

In response to a disaster, such as a major fire or flood, or before Passover when it is a tradition to clean our homes so that they are free of *ḥametz* (bread products), you can organize a "Clean Up Your Clutter Week." Ask your classmates to donate items that have become clutter for them and their families but that could be useful to someone else. Explain that this is a two-in-one mitzvah opportunity, for not only will they be helping those in need, they will also be recycling!

 **At holiday time, organize a fund-raiser for a worthy cause.** When holidays—for example, Thanksgiving, Hanukkah, Passover, and Independence Day—come around, many people are busy preparing for company and feel especially generous. It can be the perfect time to raise money with a group of friends by offering your services for a fee. For example, you might wash cars, mow lawns, rake leaves, shovel snow, or use your computer to create personalized stationery, greeting cards, or résumés for a fee.

Before you create flyers to publicize your fund-raiser, decide to whom you want the money donated. You might choose a single organization, such as the American Cancer Society, the Red Cross, or the American Friends of the Magen David Adom (Israel's equivalent of the Red Cross), or you might decide to split the proceeds, giving 50 percent to an organization that cares for people and 50 percent to one that cares for the environment. Contact the organization in advance and ask for brochures to give to your customers.

▲ When organizing a fund-raiser, you may want to involve your religious school or synagogue. For example, you can enlist their help in publicizing the project. Talk with your principal or rabbi to find out how you can work together.

 **Participate in a fund-raising sports event.** Keep in shape, have fun, and help collect tzedakah by joining members of your community in a walkathon or charity race.

▲ These participants in a muscular dystrophy walkathon are warming up before the big event. What cause would you like to support? What action can you take to help others in need?

Teens
Make a Difference
Madeline Scheffler

Madeline Scheffler is a talented cook with a heart of gold. For her bat mitzvah tzedakah project, Madeline—whose specialties include crispy potato latkes and mocha ice cream shakes—wrote a cookbook, had it printed and bound, and contributed *all* proceeds to Mazon: The Jewish Response to Hunger. (Mazon raises money within the Jewish community to feed and care for the hungry and homeless of all peoples.) Her book, *Come Cook with Me*, costs five dollars apiece to manufacture and it sells for ten dollars. Early sales figures are 300 copies sold! That's 1,500 dollars Madeline has already raised for Mazon.

On the subject of sandwiches, Madeline recommends her family's favorite: peanut butter and dill pickles. "I thought it was going to be gross, but then I tried it and loved it!" On the subject of tzedakah she says, "I am going to continue raising money until I know that I have helped many, many people." ☼

It's a Dilemma!

YOU ARE ABOUT TO PASS A PANHANDLER ON THE STREET. YOU THINK THIS MAY BE AN OPPORTUNITY TO GIVE TZEDAKAH, BUT YOU ARE CONCERNED THAT THE PERSON MAY USE THE MONEY FOR ALCOHOL, CIGARETTES, OR DRUGS RATHER THAN FOR FOOD. WHAT DO YOU DO? WHY?

_____

_____

_____

_____

_____

Self-Portrait

No two people are exactly alike. Not only do we look different from one another and have varying tastes and preferences, we also have different skills and talents. Some people are good at sports and science, while others excel in math and music. Some are terrific at organizing people, places, and things; others are good at being team players. But everybody's abilities and contributions are important.

My two most outstanding skills or talents are

_____

_____

I am proud of them because _____

_____

One way I can use them to make a difference in the

world is _____

_____

Other skills and talents I have are _____

_____

_____

They are useful to me because _____

_____

I can use them to help others by _____

_____

_____

A Holy Purpose in Not Believing

Rabbi Moshe Leib of Sassov taught, "Everything in Creation has a purpose."

Surprised, one of his students responded, "There are those who do not believe in God. Tell me, rabbi, what purpose can denying God's existence serve?"

The rabbi smiled, explaining, "When you are approached by someone in need, you must imagine that there is no God to help; you must act as if you alone can provide for the person's needs."

To deepen my commitment to the mitzvah of tzedakah, I chose to _____

_____

because _____

_____

This is what I did (provide a detailed description): _____

_____

_____

_____

I would/wouldn't choose to do this again because _____

_____

What I learned about myself by performing this mitzvah is _____

_____

_____

Of all the tzedakah projects I know about, the one I most respect is _____

_____

because _____

_____

My other thoughts on observing this mitzvah: _____

_____

_____

_____

_____

_____

④ Rodef Shalom

peacemaking

"Seek peace, and pursue it" (Psalm 34:15). The Torah does not obligate us to pursue the mitzvot, only to fulfill them at the proper time, at the appropriate occasion. Peace, however, must be sought at all times; at home and away from home, we are obligated to seek peace and pursue it.

—*Numbers Rabbah 19:27*

Although there is much that is good and beautiful in life, the world is not always a safe and peaceful place. We all know the pain of rejection and an unkind word, yet we may ridicule others or use hurtful speech. Couples promise to love each other forever; still, many fight and some divorce. Religions teach that God desires peace and loving-kindness but, all too often, people use religious beliefs to justify violence and war.

It is hard to make sense of these facts, hard to understand why we human beings find it so difficult to live in harmony with ourselves and with one another.

Our World and Our Souls Need Shalom

Inner calm, social harmony, and world peace are needed as much now as in the past. The pace of life and of change are so rapid, they can be unsettling and disruptive to our traditions and values. Jobs used to last a lifetime and families used to share the same address for generations. Farmers typically tilled the same soil their parents, grandparents, and great-grandparents had sown. Children often attended the same school and synagogue their parents and grandparents had. And generation after generation grew up on the same games, books, and music.

▲ The ancient midrash Avot de-Rebbe Natan explains: "Those who make peace in their homes are as if they made peace in all Israel." What can you do to help make your home a more peaceful and loving place?

THE WHOLE TORAH EXISTS ONLY FOR THE SAKE OF SHALOM.

–Tanḥumah, Shoftim 18

DO YOU THINK THE TORAH HAS HELPED INCREASE SHALOM IN THE WORLD? GIVE SPECIFIC EXAMPLES OR REASONS TO SUPPORT YOUR ANSWER.

_____

_____

_____

_____

Hearing the Still, Small Voice

Added to the hubbub of change is the constant barrage of the media—broadcast TV, cable TV, radio, the Internet, e-mail, "snail mail," faxes, telephones, car phones, cell phones, boom boxes....There's hardly a moment when we are alone with our own thoughts, free of the input and noise of the larger world. There is hardly any time when we can quietly settle down and listen to the still, small voice of God in our hearts.

How would you describe the voice in your heart?

_____

_____

_____

How do you keep in touch with it?

_____

_____

_____

But today we are more mobile, and our mobility often leads to fragmentation, even discord. Families often live great distances from their closest friends and relatives, challenging their identity and their sense of continuity. Adults who frequently change jobs, careers, and cities may lose sight of their youthful dreams and their core values. And popular culture changes so frequently that even brothers and sisters who are just a few years apart may experience a generation gap.

If individuals and families often feel disconnected from one another, how much more so can communities become fragmented. How much more so can peoples separated by great oceans and land masses lose sight of one another's humanity.

▲ The emblem of the modern State of Israel, shown here, includes two olive branches to symbolize Israel's yearning for shalom.

A Vision of Peace

The prophet Isaiah had a beautiful vision of a time when there would be no more wars. He wrote, "And they shall beat their swords into plowshares, and their spears into pruning hooks; nation shall not lift up sword against nation, neither shall they learn war anymore" (Isaiah 2:4).

A modern Israeli poet, Yehuda Amichai, added his own ideas to Isaiah's dream:
"Don't stop after beating the swords into plowshares, don't stop!
Go on beating and make musical instruments out of them."

In this space, write a poem or draw a picture of your vision of what the world will be like when there is no more war.

Shalom—the Heart and Soul of Judaism

The mitzvah of *rodef shalom* is the act of pursuing peace in ourselves, in our homes, in our communities, and in the larger world. It is at the heart and soul of Judaism. Every major Jewish prayer ends with a petition for peace. The first book of rabbinic law and wisdom, the Mishnah, ends with a prayer for peace. And a volume of the Talmud—*Perek Hashalom* (The Chapter of Peace)—is entirely devoted to the subject of peace.

Peace Is Always in Our Prayers

WHEN WE RECITE THE AMIDAH, WE PRAY THAT GOD WILL "GRANT PEACE TO THE WORLD, WITH GOODNESS AND BLESSING, GRACE, LOVE, AND MERCY." DURING FRIDAY NIGHT SERVICES WE RECITE THE HASHKIVEINU PRAYER AND IMPLORE GOD TO "SPREAD OVER US THE SHELTER OF YOUR PEACE." AND WHEN WE RECITE THE BIRKAT HAMAZON, THE GRACE AFTER MEALS, WE ASK THAT GOD "CAUSE PEACE TO DWELL AMONG US."

▲ Prayer can provide quiet moments in which to hear the still, small voice of God.

Symbols of shalom are deeply woven into the fabric of Jewish tradition. Shabbat is known as a day of peace that celebrates harmony among people, God, and nature. The Temple in Jerusalem was a monument to peace at which Jews would pray for their own well-being and that of the other nations of the world. Finally, the most prominent religious leader in biblical Judaism, the *Kohen Gadol* (High Priest), became a symbol of peace and an instrument for its achievement.

An essential goal of living as an adult Jew is to sow seeds of peace within yourself, your family, and your community, as well as in the larger world. Our tradition can be a source of inspiration and wisdom that helps you achieve this goal.

SHALOM IS MORE THAN PEACE

The ancient Greek word for "peace" simply means the opposite of war, and the Roman goddess Pax ("Peace") was a minor deity until the time of the Roman Empire. But from the time of the Bible onward, the word *shalom* has carried a wealth of positive meanings. Not merely indicating the absence of war, *shalom* means "safety," "wholeness," "completion," "fulfillment," "prosperity," "health," and "peace of mind and heart." Shalom is even one of God's names!

think about it!

JEWISH TRADITION TEACHES THAT *rodef shalom*, SEEKING PEACE, IS A HOLY ACT. WHEN YOU AVOID UNNECESSARY ARGUMENTS AT HOME OR HELP YOUR FRIENDS SETTLE THEIR DISAGREEMENTS, YOU ARE PREPARING YOURSELF TO BE A PEACEMAKER. HOW ELSE CAN YOU PREPARE TO BECOME A PEACEMAKER? HOW CAN PURSUING PEACE HELP YOU BECOME A RESPONSIBLE CITIZEN AND JEW?

The word *shalom* comes from the same root as *shalem*, which means "whole" or "complete." Judaism teaches that we must pursue peace to complete ourselves and to help bring wholeness to our families, communities, and the larger world. Here are some ways you can fulfill the mitzvah of *rodef shalom*.

Ready! Set! GO!

Help make your home a peaceful place. The origin of peace is in the home; consequently, Jewish tradition stresses the importance of *sh'lom bayit* (peace in the home). By learning to live peaceably with those you love (which may be more difficult than it sounds), you establish a pocket of shalom that can spread beyond the confines of your home.

Seek inner calm and strength. There is no single place where you can go to attain inner peace, no one person or group that can confer it on you. But by gradually becoming more self-aware, more tolerant, and more willing to work toward self-improvement, you can gain the peace and satisfaction of loving and respecting yourself and of enjoying your own company. Here are two suggestions that can help you.

◆ *Find a quiet corner and read* Sefer Tehillim *(the Book of Psalms)*. For thousands of years, Jews (and, later, Christians) have found great comfort from reading this book of poetry. Among the psalms you may find personal favorites to which you can return for strength and comfort.

◆ *Keep a diary.* Record random thoughts, reactions, and dreams. A diary or journal is a useful tool for tracing and exploring inner growth in a way that is safe, private, and honest.

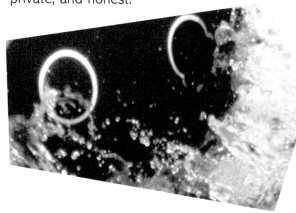

▲ If you feel like telling someone to go jump in a lake, it may be time for you to cool off and do it yourself!

Like inner peace, *sh'lom bayit* requires respect for others. From time to time, family members disappoint one another (as we all disappoint ourselves at moments). But as long as we are self-disciplined enough to listen to others' needs and points of view, and as long as we work hard to improve our behavior, then *sh'lom bayit* will be a realistic goal.

 **Develop your conflict-resolution skills.** Here are a few tips for resolving differences of opinion.

♦ *Try to remain calm.* You are unlikely to be heard if you shout.

♦ *Don't engage in put-downs.* It won't get you what you want; instead, it will probably make the other person even more distrustful and defensive.

♦ *Don't interrupt others.* Build respect by letting others finish speaking. (This will also make them more likely to let you finish what you have to say.)

♦ *Listen to what others have to say.* Don't get so caught up in planning your response that you can't hear the concerns of other people or the legitimacy of their points of view.

♦ *Be patient.* If you cannot resolve a conflict, suggest that you each give things a rest and return to the issue at a later time.

 **Ask yourself, "Do I view violent acts as entertainment?"** Every day, in almost every American home, murders, beatings, violent explosions, kidnappings, and other horrors make their way into family rooms, dens, and living rooms through "entertainment centers." The effect of witnessing this mayhem? In a review of thirty-three studies on the effect of televised violence, thirty-one demonstrated that children behave more aggressively after viewing violence. They are more likely to hit other children, call people names, and refuse to obey classroom or parental instruction.

▲ Sometimes when we are upset, it helps to cool off by doing something we enjoy or finding a quiet place to relax.

Consider taking the following steps:

♦ *Change the channel or shut the set off if there is violence on TV.* There is no substitute for direct action and, if you want to make a difference, there's no better place to start taking action than in your own home.

♦ *Write to your congressional representative and senators, expressing your disapproval.* While you may have serious concerns about free speech and a wise mistrust of censorship, remember that decisions about which programs to air are often based on which can bring in the greatest number of advertising dollars, rather than on which can contribute to a healthy citizenry. As a result, many worthwhile shows never make the "fall lineup."

Self-Portrait

⭐ Being aware of how you react when you are upset or under pressure can help you decide which behaviors you want to avoid in the future and with which coping strategies you want to replace them.

⭐ When I'm angry or stressed-out, I:
(Check as many responses as are appropriate)

_____ WRITE IN MY DIARY   _____ EAT, EAT, EAT

_____ SMOKE CIGARETTES   _____ LISTEN TO LOUD MUSIC

_____ CALL A FRIEND   _____ WATCH TV

_____ EXERCISE   _____ CRY

_____ PLAY VIDEO GAMES   _____ WITHDRAW

_____ SURF THE NET   _____ TAKE A SHOWER

OTHER: _____

⭐ I feel comfortable/uncomfortable continuing

to handle stress and anger by _____

BECAUSE _____

_____

⭐ A coping strategy I admire in others is

_____

BECAUSE _____

_____

⭐ One change I would like to make to improve my

ability to cope with problems is _____

_____

It's a Dilemma!

Let's be honest—every family has its problems and conflicts. The Torah doesn't ask us to deny these concerns, it only requires that we do our best to address them in a peaceful and loving way.

Lots of teens say their parents ask them to do something—a chore, homework, an errand—just when they are ready to relax or call a friend. Does this ever happen to you? Think about what you can do or say to avoid escalating the request into a conflict.

What I can do to avoid such conflicts in the future:

_____

_____

_____

What I'd like my parents to do in the future:

_____

_____

_____

How I'll let them know:

_____

_____

_____

think about it!

Ironically, most people find that the more patient and loving they are toward others, the more love and care they have for themselves. Do you think this is true for you? Why or why not?

First [one] should put [one's] house together, then [one's] town, then the world."
—*Rabbi Israel Salanter*

Do you agree or disagree with this statement? Why?

_____

_____

_____

_____

_____

_____

_____

_____

▲ Abraham Joshua Heschel, a rabbi, scholar, and social activist, joined the civil rights movement because he believed it was "a way of worshipping God." Heschel is shown (front, second from right) marching from Selma to Montgomery, Alabama, in 1965, along with (from his right) Ralph Bunche, Martin Luther King, Jr., and Ralph Abernathy.

5 **Talk about prejudice in groups that include people who often encounter such hostility.**
For example, you might include people of color and people with special needs. These discussions can be organized through youth organizations, such as United Synagogue Youth (USY), North American Federation of Temple Youth (NFTY), and Young Judaea. For those who live in an area with a large Jewish population, the local Jewish federation often sponsors a Jewish community relations council that organizes small, informal discussions among different religious and ethnic groups.

6 **Become aware of the issues related to peace on an international level and take action.**
Join an organization such as 20/20 Vision, which educates people on the issues affecting world peace and suggests specific steps members can take. Each month, 20/20 Vision mails a postcard to its members asking that they take a specific action—make a phone call or write a short letter. It summarizes the issue and the points to make and provides the name and address of the person or organization to contact. The cost of membership is twenty dollars per year, and the organization promises that it will require only twenty minutes of your time each month.

◀ Do you think that video games that portray violence have a negative impact on teens who play them? Why or why not?

7. Correspond with a pen pal.

Establishing a correspondence with someone in another country puts a human face on a distant part of the globe—and shows the humanity in our own little corner.

▲ Yitzhak Rabin was a military commander who served in the defense of Israel for 27 years and then became prime minister. In 1995 he was assassinated by a Jewish religious fanatic who opposed the peace process Rabin supported.

Sense or Censorship?

A recent nationwide survey of more than 218,000 sixth through twelfth graders found that 30 percent believe that restrictions should be placed on teens' Internet access, and 35 percent feel that it's okay for parents to block offensive or violent TV programs.

Do you agree or disagree—that is, do you think it makes sense or is it unreasonable censorship? Why?

_____

_____

_____

_____

_____

_____

_____

_____

Shabbat Shalom!

ONE WAY TO REMIND YOURSELF OF THE IMPORTANCE JUDAISM PLACES ON SHALOM IS TO USE THE TRADITIONAL WORDS FOR SAYING HELLO AND GOOD-BYE ON THE HOLIEST DAY OF THE WEEK—*Shabbat shalom!*

TO BLAME OR NOT TO BLAME

When there is a conflict, people often think more about who is to blame than about how to improve the situation. Try not to resolve conflicts by assigning blame or by trying to prove that you are right. Instead, make an effort to understand the other person's point of view and help that person understand yours, including how you feel and what you want. Sometimes, when others understand you better and you understand them, conflicts don't seem so insurmountable.

Psychologists have found that making "I statements" can reduce conflict. A formula that can help you communicate better is:

"I feel _____

when _____

because_____

I want you to _____ "

When trying to resolve a conflict, you need to decide which is more important to you—being right or improving the relationship.

After negotiating a peace arrangement, called the Declaration of Principles, with Yasir Arafat, chairman of the Palestine Liberation Organization, Israeli prime minister Yitzhak Rabin commented, "I would have liked to sign a peace agreement with Holland, or Luxembourg, or New Zealand. But there was no need to. ...One does not make peace with one's friends. One makes peace with one's enemy."

What do you think Rabin meant?

_____
_____
_____
_____
_____
_____

How might this apply to your life?

_____
_____
_____
_____
_____
_____
_____

To deepen my commitment to the mitzvah of *rodef shalom*, I chose to _____

_____

because _____

_____

This is what I did (provide a detailed description): _____

_____

_____

_____

I would/wouldn't choose to do this again because _____

_____

One way I can increase *sh'lom bayit* is _____

_____ because _____

_____

_____

What I learned about myself by performing this mitzvah is _____

_____

My other thoughts on observing this mitzvah: _____

_____

_____

_____

_____

_____

_____

⑤ Shabbat

an extraordinary day

Remember the Shabbat day to keep it holy.

—*Exodus 20:8*

Every seven days, for one full day, starting at sundown on Friday evening and lasting until the light of the first three stars is visible on Saturday night, the Jewish people—and all who wish to join us—are bid to leave the hustle and bustle of daily life to enter Shabbat, God's Palace in Time.

A Time of Greater Freedom

Shabbat is an oasis in the week, a full day free from daily concerns, free from stress, and free from the demands of school, chores, and achievement. Shabbat is also much, much more. It is the time given to us to renew our bodies and our spirits; draw closer to our families, our community, and our God; and refocus on both our personal and our Jewish values and priorities. Undistracted from the need to produce or to do, we can let Shabbat teach us how to strengthen our personal relationships, as well as how to rededicate ourselves to making the weekday world a more just, more compassionate and therefore more godly place.

A Gift and a Choice

As attractive a gift as Shabbat is, as tempting as freedom and renewal are, it is not always easy to draw our weekday activities to a close. Sometimes we keep on going, doing just a bit more and then a bit more after that. Before we know it, the entire day is gone. And then, perhaps, another Shabbat. Gradually we may become enslaved by our work, our obligations, even our play.

But if we allow our work and other commitments to control us, it is we who must accept responsibility. Shabbat is there for the taking; however, it cannot grab us in a choke hold, forcing us to accept the freedom it offers.

⭐ FOR ME, TIME FEELS HOLY WHEN I AM: (CHECK AS MANY RESPONSES AS ARE APPROPRIATE)

_____ WITH FRIENDS

_____ WITH FAMILY

_____ WITH COMMUNITY

_____ ALONE

_____ SINGING

_____ EATING

_____ PRAYING

_____ PLAYING A MUSICAL INSTRUMENT

_____ READING

_____ STUDYING TORAH

_____ EXERCISING

_____ LISTENING TO MUSIC

_____ MEDITATING

_____ HELPING OTHERS

_____ RELAXING

_____ OBSERVING RELIGIOUS HOLIDAYS

OTHER: _____

_____

Shabbat is a gift of choice. Therefore, we must *choose* to switch gears, *choose* to declare the day and ourselves holy, *choose* to join others in celebration. If we do not, Friday night and Saturday will remain ordinary, and the holiness of Shabbat will remain beyond our reach.

▲ Sometimes, you may be shy about asserting your need to leave a group activity, such as team sports or band practice, in order to get ready for Shabbat. But put the shoe on the other foot. If a Muslim or Christian had a religious need that conflicted with the group's plan, wouldn't you be respectful? Why not assume that others would be as open to your needs?

WHAT WAS CREATED ON THE SEVENTH DAY?

Genesis 2:2 states: "On the seventh day God finished the work [of Creation]." Our sages asked—and answered—an interesting question, "What was created after it was already Shabbat? Tranquility, serenity, peace, and quiet" (*Genesis Rabbah 17:7*).

Ready! Set! GO!

Here are some suggestions on how to observe Shabbat—how to transport yourself from the ordinariness of the school week into the holiness of Shabbat. The blessings and songs that are listed can be found in most Shabbat prayer books. Check the table of contents of your synagogue's siddur.

1 **Wear special clothes.** It is a tradition to bathe and to change clothes before the start of Shabbat. It is also a tradition to dress in a way that helps make the evening distinctive and pleasurable.

2 **Light Shabbat candles and recite the blessing over the candles.** Use the ritual as an opportunity to bring your family together. After concluding the blessing, take a moment to reflect on the events of the week, on the people who help make your life worthwhile, and on the warmth and beauty of the candles. Enjoy their glow.

3 **Make your Friday night meal special.** Suggest to your family that you set the table with a tablecloth (white if possible), holiday dishes and cutlery, and a bouquet of flowers. Include two loaves of ḥallah, covered by a decorative cloth or napkin, and a

▲ This Shabbat outfit was worn in Europe in the 19th century. What can you wear on Shabbat to help make the day distinctive?

Kiddush cup or other attractive glass. (Some families provide each person with his or her own Kiddush cup, while others use one cup that is shared by everyone.)

◆ *Begin the meal with everyone singing "Shalom Aleichem."* This can be sung while all hold hands around the table or place their arms on the shoulders of those who are seated next to them.

◆ *Recite the Kiddush (literally, "Sanctification").* This prayer sanctifies the beginning of Shabbat. It recalls the Creation of the world and our ancestors' Exodus from Egypt.

◆ *Recite Hamotzi, the blessing over bread.* Then pass the ḥallah around so that everyone can tear off a piece. Once you have eaten some ḥallah, you are ready to enjoy both the company and the meal. Traditional Shabbat meals often include special foods, such as gefilte fish, potato or noodle pudding (kugel), and chicken with pomegranates, nuts, and rice, a Middle Eastern dish.

◆ *Sing Shabbat z'mirot (songs).* This adds to the festive mood of the meal and provides an activity in which people of all ages can participate. In addition to Hebrew z'mirot such as "Oseh Shalom" and "Lo Yisa Goy El Goy," you may want to sing English songs of freedom and peace, such as "We Shall Overcome" and "Down by the Riverside." Ask your teacher or principal where you can get a songster with Shabbat z'mirot.

◆ *Recite the Birkat Hamazon (Grace After Meals).* While it is appropriate to recite the Birkat Hamazon after every meal, you may want to begin by making it a Shabbat practice, both as a way of developing the habit and as a means of making Shabbat special.

▶ On Shabbat, the Torah reading service reminds us of the traditions and values we want to guide our lives.

▲ Shabbat adds a sweetness and a rhythm to the week. All that is needed to begin observing this day of rest are two white candles, wine or grape juice, two loaves of ḥallah, and a tasty meal with family and friends.

4 **Invite guests for Shabbat dinner or lunch, or for dessert on Shabbat afternoon.** Invite a relative, a friend, or a potential friend from school or synagogue to help you enjoy the day. Shabbat won't feel isolating if it becomes a time to enjoy the company of other people, to strengthen ties to your extended family and the community, or to establish new friendships.

5 **Attend Friday night and/or Saturday morning synagogue services.** Invite your friends and family to join you. On Shabbat we are asked to draw closer to God, our families, and our community. The synagogue provides the meeting place, and the prayer service provides the words of love, hope, and gratitude that bind us together.

▲ Spending time with younger siblings or cousins on Shabbat can be a big treat for them and an opportunity for you to strengthen family ties.

Also consider playing a ball game near your home, throwing a Frisbee, going for a run with a friend, or enjoying a non-competitive athletic activity. The advantage of participating in athletics on Shabbat is that your focus is limited to pleasure and health. Competition and concern for status, which so often motivate athletic performance on other days, are best set aside on Shabbat. The focus of the day should be one of pleasure for its own sake.

▼ Just as Shabbat begins with a candle-lighting ceremony, so does it end with one.

▲ The prohibitions against working on Shabbat are meant to free us from the drudgery of our daily lives. The luxury of free time can enable us to play in the park, take a Shabbat nap or stroll, exercise, read, and enjoy the company of others.

6 Limit your Shabbat activities to those of menuḥah (literally, "rest"). There are several kinds of menuḥah. One form is leisure activities, such as reading a magazine or book. Another form of menuḥah is a Shabbat stroll. Alone or with someone else, enjoy a leisurely walk as you explore your own or a nearby neighborhood.

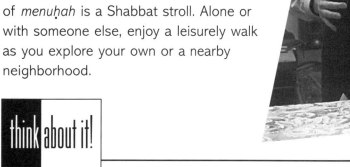

think about it!

ON SHABBAT, THE NATURAL ORDER OF THE WORLD IS THE SAME AS IT IS SUNDAY THROUGH FRIDAY. THE SUN RISES AND SETS AS IT ALWAYS DOES. PINE TREES REMAIN GREEN AND THE SKY, BLUE. BIRDS CONTINUE TO FLY, SNAKES TO CRAWL, AND FISH TO SWIM. THE DIFFERENCE ON SHABBAT IS THE DIFFERENCE IN US—THE JEWISH PEOPLE.

HOW WILL YOU MAKE A DIFFERENCE ON SHABBAT? HOW CAN YOU HELP MAKE SHABBAT A HOLY DAY, A PALACE IN TIME?

Yet another form of *menuḥah* involves sacred study for relaxation and pleasure, either alone or with others. Shabbat afternoon is an ideal time to read and discuss the weekly Torah portion, perhaps even a little Talmud.

Additionally, you might discuss a news item that raises issues of justice, compassion, or faith, and consider how the Torah's teachings might add to your insights. Alternatively, you may choose to read a Jewish newspaper or a book on Jewish history, religion, or philosophy.

 **Perform the Havdalah ceremony.** *Havdalah* (literally, "differentiation") marks our return to the workaday world. For this ritual, you will need a braided candle with at least two wicks. (*Havdalah* candles are sold in synagogue and Judaica shops.) You will also need a spice box and at least two spices (cloves and cinnamon are the two most frequently used spices, although any pleasant smelling spices are fine), some kosher wine or grape juice, and an attractive glass or Kiddush cup.

▲ Havdalah candle in holder

It's a Dilemma!

ELIE WIESEL, A JEWISH NOBEL PEACE PRIZE WINNER, WAS INVITED TO THROW OUT THE FIRST BALL OF THE 1986 WORLD SERIES. HE THANKED THE BASEBALL COMMISSIONER BUT SAID HE COULD NOT ACCEPT THE HONOR BECAUSE THE GAME WAS ON SHABBAT, A HOLY DAY.

THE COMMISSIONER WAS SO IMPRESSED BY WIESEL'S RESPECT FOR THE SABBATH THAT HE INVITED HIM TO THROW OUT THE FIRST BALL OF THE SECOND GAME, WHICH WAS HELD ON A WEEKDAY. PLEASED, ELIE WIESEL ACCEPTED.

SIMILARLY, SENATOR JOSEPH LIEBERMAN, AN OBSERVANT JEW WHO RECEIVED THE DEMOCRATIC NOMINATION FOR THE VICE PRESIDENCY OF THE UNITED STATES IN 2000, PROVED THAT IT IS POSSIBLE TO OBSERVE SHABBAT *and* TO FULLY PARTICIPATE IN AMERICAN LIFE.

EACH OF US SOMETIMES FACES DILEMMAS ABOUT HOW TO JUGGLE OUR RELIGIOUS COMMITMENTS AND IDEALS WITH OUR OTHER OBLIGATIONS AND DESIRES. WHAT DILEMMAS DO YOU FACE IN OBSERVING SHABBAT?

_____
_____
_____

HOW MIGHT YOU RESOLVE SOME OF THEM?

_____
_____
_____
_____

"Even more than the Jews have kept Shabbat, Shabbat has kept the Jews."
—*Aḥad Ha'am*

What do you think Aḥad Ha'am meant? Why might this be so?

_____

_____

_____

_____

Do you think this is true in your community? in your family? Why?

_____

_____

_____

_____

_____

_____

The Legend Of The Two Angels

The words of "Shalom Aleichem" are based on a Talmudic legend about two angels—one good, the other evil. According to the legend, if the angels see that a family is enjoying a loving Shabbat meal, then the good angel can coerce the evil one to wish that all future Shabbat meals will be this wonderful.

The Freedom to Observe Mitzvot

On Shabbat we remember our ancestors' liberation from slavery in Egypt. Slaves can't decide when they will work and when they will rest. Thus, they cannot fulfill the mitzvah of observing Shabbat. Only a free person can observe Shabbat.

What other mitzvot can only be observed by free people?

_____

_____

Why do you think so?

_____

_____

Getting Into The Spirit Of Shabbat

Each Friday, before lighting Shabbat candles, it is a tradition to donate tzedakah. You can buy a tzedakah box or make one using a container you decorate. Then once or twice a year, perhaps on your birthday and right before Yom Kippur or Passover, you can donate the money to a favorite cause. Here are some other ways to get into the spirit of Shabbat.

- Call or e-mail a grandparent and other relatives, a friend, or someone else who would appreciate hearing from you.
- Clean your room.
- Help with the household chores or preparation of the Shabbat meal.

How will you get into the spirit of Shabbat?

To deepen my commitment to the mitzvah of observing Shabbat, I chose to _____

_____

because _____

_____

This is what I did (provide a detailed description): _____

_____

_____

_____

I would/wouldn't choose to do this again because _____

_____

The most difficult thing about stopping my weekday activities on Shabbat is _____

_____

because _____

_____

The best thing about Shabbat is _____

_____

My other thoughts on observing this mitzvah: _____

_____

_____

_____

_____

_____

_____

⑥ Ahavat Tziyon

for the love of Israel

The Jewish People...forced to leave their ancient country, has never abandoned, never forsaken, the Holy Land; the Jewish People has never ceased to be passionate about Zion. It has always lived in a dialogue with the Holy Land.

—Rabbi Abraham Joshua Heschel

Suppose your family attended synagogue services not only with the members of your congregation, but also with all your Jewish friends and relatives: friends from summer camp and from music lessons, from school and from sports; and all your grandmothers, grandfathers, and all your aunts, uncles, and cousins. Where would you go for these services?

Now imagine that every Jew in the world gathered in one place to pray, to celebrate Passover, or to create an action plan to care for the environment or to help those suffering from poverty or disease. Where do you think the best place for such a gathering would be? Why?

Israel would be the most natural choice for all these gatherings. For Israel is the homeland of the Jewish people. To us, it is not only the holiest parcel of land on Earth, it is also where we first dreamed our most extraordinary dream of a complete and perfect world, a world in which there is no hunger, war, or hatred—a world in which God's commandments are fulfilled and all God's creatures live in peace. It is in Israel that we first dared to be our best selves and first accepted responsibility to help others succeed as well.

THE HEBREW WORD *Yisrael* MEANS "TO STRUGGLE WITH GOD AND SUCCEED." *Yisrael*, THE NAME OF BOTH OUR PEOPLE AND OUR HOLY LAND, REMINDS US THAT THE JEWISH TRADITION IS ONE OF STRUGGLE AND COURAGE. OUR STRUGGLE IS TO LIVE AS A HOLY PEOPLE—*am kadosh*. THROUGHOUT THE GENERATIONS, OUR COURAGE HAS COME FROM GOD, OUR COMMUNITY, AND THE WISDOM OF OUR TRADITION.

THINK ABOUT A MOMENT OR EVENT IN WHICH BEING JEWISH PRESENTED A PROBLEM OR A STRUGGLE FOR YOU. WHAT HAPPENED? HOW DID YOU DEAL WITH IT? _____

_____

_____

_____

ONE THING I STRUGGLE WITH ABOUT BEING JEWISH IS _____

_____

BECAUSE _____

_____

I GAIN COURAGE WHEN I: (CHECK AS MANY CHOICES AS ARE APPROPRIATE)

_____ THINK ABOUT PEOPLE WHO
OVERCAME GREAT DIFFICULTIES

_____ TALK WITH MY FRIENDS

_____ TALK WITH MY FAMILY

_____ PRAY WITH THE COMMUNITY

_____ THINK ABOUT THE JEWS WHO
CAME BEFORE ME

_____ PRAY BY MYSELF

_____ STUDY JEWISH HISTORY

_____ STUDY TORAH

OTHER: _____

_____

_____

The Promise of the Holy Land

The Torah teaches that God promised the Land of Canaan (which is what Israel was called in ancient times) to Abraham and Sarah for their family and descendants. God's promise is repeated many times in the Torah; thus, Israel became known as the Promised Land.

The Torah also teaches that God fulfilled this promise by delivering our ancestors from slavery and bringing them to the place where they were first able to live according to God's commandments. Indeed, the Land of Israel, *Eretz Yisrael*, is the home of some of the holiest places and events in Jewish history. That is why we also call it our Holy Land.

The patriarchs—Abraham, Isaac, and Jacob—and the matriarchs—Sarah, Rebecca, Rachel, and Leah—lived in *Eretz Yisrael*. Deborah, Yael, and Gideon defended Israel against its enemies. King Saul, King David, and King Solomon reigned over Israel. And Jeremiah, Amos, and Isaiah were prophets in Israel. The Holy Temple where our ancestors prayed was built in the Land of Israel—in Jerusalem, the holiest city in the world for Jews. And Hebrew—the holy language of Torah—was spoken by our ancestors in *Eretz Yisrael*.

▶ **Deborah was a prophetess and a military leader in ancient Israel. Her story is told in the Book of Judges.**

A Tradition of Courage and Struggle

When the Romans conquered the Land of Israel almost 2,000 years ago, most Jews were exiled. But they carried the Torah with them to the four corners of the earth. Each generation passed the teachings of the Torah and of our sages on to the next. And each generation prayed that we would once again live in *Eretz Yisrael*, as a holy people in our own land.

Through the centuries, there have been many other exiled peoples who have also been forced to leave their homelands. But in time, each group dispersed and ceased to be a people, for without a country they lost the will to stay together. Jews are the only exiled nation that has remained one people, even though we had to wait 2,000 years to return to our Holy Land.

◀ In 1985, the Jewish communities of Israel and North America saved the Jews of Ethiopia from oppression and famine in a dramatic airlift that brought them to freedom in Israel. The airlift was called "Operation Moses." Whatever the differences among Jews, we share one Torah and one homeland, Israel.

The Modern State of Israel

In the late 19th century, a group of Jews recognized the need for a Jewish state to ensure Jewish liberty. Led by journalist Theodor Herzl (1860–1904), these activists created a political movement dedicated to establishing a Jewish government on Jewish soil. Herzl and the other activists called themselves Zionists, people who believe in the right of the Jewish people to exist as a free and sovereign nation on its own soil. But it was not until May 14, 1948—after mobilizing the support of Jews around the globe, after many appeals to the world community, and after much bloodshed—that the modern State of Israel, *Medinat Yisrael*, was born. Finally, we had a state of our own—a place where Jews would always be welcome.

Survivors of the Holocaust came from Europe to begin new lives. Jews also came from North African and Arab countries, such as Morocco and Iraq, where for centuries they had lived in poverty and danger. Others came from America and Canada.

The establishment of *Medinat Yisrael* breathed new life into the Jewish people. It restored our pride and our strength as schools, libraries, synagogues, hospitals, and museums were built, and the desert was made to bloom through irrigation and the planting of trees and fields.

THEODOR HERZL'S SLOGAN WAS: "IF YOU WILL IT, IT IS NO DREAM." WHAT DO YOU THINK IT MEANS TO WILL SOMETHING?_____

_____

_____

_____

_____

DO YOU HAVE DREAMS THAT YOU HAVE WILLED INTO COMING TRUE? IF SO, WHAT DID YOU DO TO MAKE THEM HAPPEN?

_____

_____

_____

_____

_____

It's a Dilemma!

IN 1948, JEWS AROUND THE WORLD CELE-
BRATED THE CREATION OF *Medinat Yisrael*,
BUT NO ONE KNEW EXACTLY WHAT A MODERN
JEWISH STATE SHOULD BE LIKE. SHOULD ONLY
JEWS BE CITIZENS? SHOULD THE PRIME MIN-
ISTER BE A RABBI? WHAT HOLIDAYS SHOULD
BE CELEBRATED AS NATIONAL HOLIDAYS?

EVEN TODAY, NOT EVERYONE HAS THE SAME
OPINION. EVIDENCE OF THIS IS SEEN IN THE
TENSION THAT SOMETIMES FLARES UP
BETWEEN SECULAR JEWS, OBSERVANT BUT
NON-ORTHODOX JEWS, AND STRICTLY
ORTHODOX JEWS (*haredim*). FOR INSTANCE,
MANY *haredim* HAVE FOUGHT TO CLOSE MOVIE
THEATERS ON SHABBAT, AND SOME *haredim*
BLOCK ROADS SO THAT OTHER JEWS CANNOT
DRIVE THROUGH THEIR NEIGHBORHOODS ON
SHABBAT.

DO YOU THINK THE GOVERNMENT OF A
JEWISH STATE SHOULD REQUIRE JEWS TO
OBSERVE SHABBAT WHEN THEY ARE IN PUBLIC
PLACES? WHY OR WHY NOT?

_____

_____

_____

_____

IF YOUR ANSWER IS YES, HOW DO YOU
GUARANTEE FREEDOM? IF IT IS NO, HOW DO
YOU GUARANTEE THE JEWISHNESS OF THE
STATE OF ISRAEL?

_____

_____

_____

Our Commitment to Israel

One of the most remarkable achievements
of the Jewish people has been our continued
devotion to *Eretz Yisrael*. That love is not only
a shared passion; it is a mitzvah, the mitzvah
of *ahavat Tziyon*, or love of Zion. The prophet
Isaiah records the command "Rejoice with
Jerusalem and be glad for her" (66:10), and
Psalm 137:5–6 speaks for the Jewish people
when pledging:

If I forget you, O Jerusalem, let my right
hand wither.

Let my tongue cleave to my palate if I stop
thinking of you,

If I do not set Jerusalem above my
greatest joy.

▲ The Tel Aviv Museum exhibits
the work of artists from Israel and
around the world.

think about it!

DO YOU THINK IT IS NECESSARY TO FEEL
CONNECTED TO ISRAEL? DO YOU THINK LOVE
OF ISRAEL HELPS JEWS AROUND THE WORLD
REMAIN AS ONE COMMUNITY? WHY OR WHY
NOT?

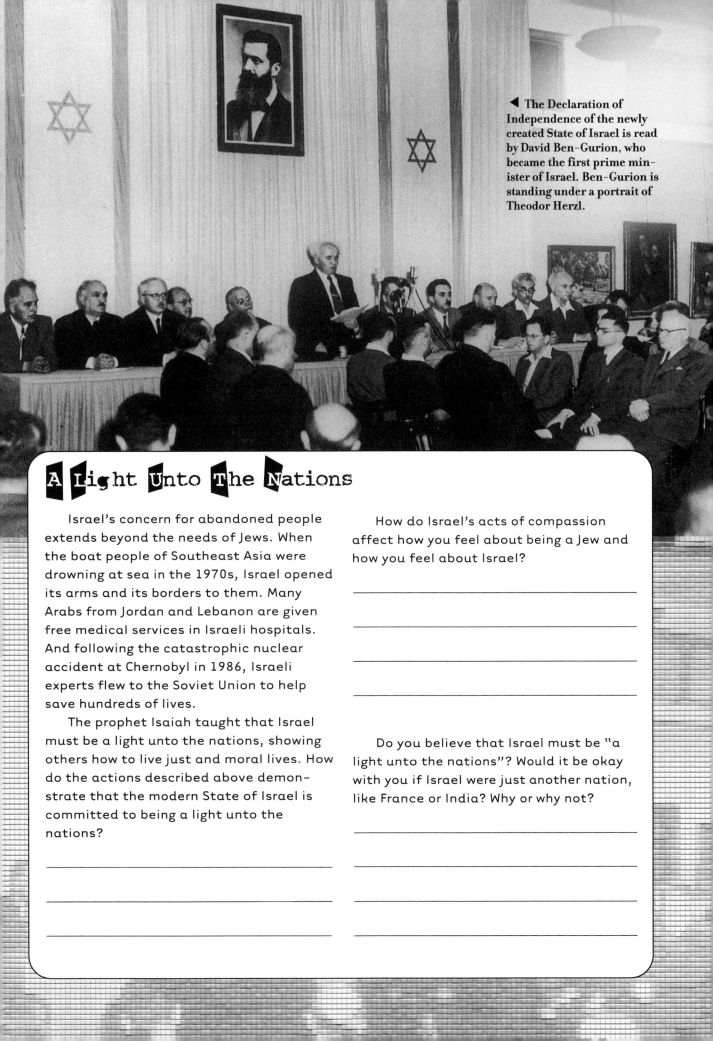

◄ The Declaration of Independence of the newly created State of Israel is read by David Ben-Gurion, who became the first prime minister of Israel. Ben-Gurion is standing under a portrait of Theodor Herzl.

A Light Unto The Nations

Israel's concern for abandoned people extends beyond the needs of Jews. When the boat people of Southeast Asia were drowning at sea in the 1970s, Israel opened its arms and its borders to them. Many Arabs from Jordan and Lebanon are given free medical services in Israeli hospitals. And following the catastrophic nuclear accident at Chernobyl in 1986, Israeli experts flew to the Soviet Union to help save hundreds of lives.

The prophet Isaiah taught that Israel must be a light unto the nations, showing others how to live just and moral lives. How do the actions described above demonstrate that the modern State of Israel is committed to being a light unto the nations?

_____

_____

_____

How do Israel's acts of compassion affect how you feel about being a Jew and how you feel about Israel?

_____

_____

_____

_____

Do you believe that Israel must be "a light unto the nations"? Would it be okay with you if Israel were just another nation, like France or India? Why or why not?

_____

_____

_____

Israel's diversity often surprises those who know how small the country is. From the natural beauty of its mountains, fields, forests, coral reefs, and beaches, to the ancient remains of the biblical and rabbinic past, to the modern metropolis of Tel Aviv, Israel is a marvel on many levels.

Here are some ways you can fulfill the mitzvah of *ahavat Tziyon*.

Ready! Set! GO!

1 **Keep up with Israeli current events.** Begin by reading any newspaper or magazine article about Israel or the Middle East. Gradually, the many names, political parties, and geographic locations will begin to make more sense. Then, make it a habit to search the Internet for news on Israel and subscribe to an English-language Israeli newspaper or magazine, or check out your synagogue's library to see if it has a subscription.

For many American Jews, Israel means military conflict, Jewish political parties, and rabbis arguing about legislation. But this ignores how Israeli literature, education, sports, and art produce exciting expressions of what it means to live as a Jew in the modern world.

Two excellent English-language publications are the *Jerusalem Post, International Edition* (a weekly Israeli newspaper) and *The Jerusalem Report* (a magazine), which offer broad coverage of Israeli politics and culture as well as reports on Jewish news from around the world. Reading them can also keep you up-to-date on what's happening with Israeli teens—the latest rock stars, movies, and fashions.

2 **Collect Israeli music.** There are many talented Israeli singers and musicians who perform a wide range of music—Israeli folk, jazz, rock, world pop, cantorial, and classical.

▲ Yael Arad, Israeli Olympic medalist

Many North American cities have Judaica shops that carry Israeli music as well as books and ritual items; some recordings are even available in general music stores, through Judaica direct-mail catalogs, and online.

Buy Israeli products. A Shabbat dinner can feature Israeli wine, and many salads will improve with the addition of Israeli tomatoes and seedless cucumbers. Israeli swimsuits are among the most fashionable in the world, and Judaic crafts—such as ceramic or silver Kiddush cups and Ḥanukkah menorahs—make unique and beautiful gifts. Encourage your family to buy Israeli products as a way to both help Israel's economy and strengthen a personal connection to the Jewish homeland.

▲ If your synagogue has a gift shop, check it out. Its Israeli crafts could make perfect Ḥanukkah, anniversary, or bat or bar mitzvah gifts.

Help rebuild Israel's land by planting trees. By planting millions of trees and carefully tending the soil, Israel has revitalized fertile land that had become desert. The driving force behind this effort has been the Jewish National Fund (JNF). The JNF organizes massive tree plantings and provides equipment and machinery to maintain and cultivate land in Israel. Parks, settlements, homes, and nature preserves have mushroomed in Israel because of JNF's efforts. Here are two simple ways to help make a difference in the Land of Israel:

Israeli Sports Heroes

IF YOU LIKE TO KEEP UP WITH THE WORLD OF SPORTS, YOU WILL FIND THAT ISRAELI ATHLETES ARE BIG NEWS!

- TAL BRODY, BORN IN TRENTON, NEW JERSEY, WAS OFFERED THE CHANCE TO PLAY PROFESSIONAL BASKETBALL FOR THE BALTIMORE BULLETS IN 1965. INSTEAD, HE LED THE U.S. TEAM TO THE GOLD MEDAL IN THE ISRAELI MACCABIAH GAMES. TAL RETURNED TO LIVE IN ISRAEL IN 1970, JOINING THE MACCABI TEL AVIV BASKETBALL TEAM. HE HAS INTRODUCED NUMEROUS ISRAELI CHILDREN TO BASKETBALL THROUGH HIS AFTER-SCHOOL PROGRAM, "LET'S PLAY BALL!"

- YAEL ARAD WON ISRAEL'S FIRST OLYMPIC MEDAL, A SILVER, IN THE 1992 BARCELONA OLYMPICS IN THE WOMEN'S 61-KILO CLASS JUDO EVENT.

- KEREN LEIBOWITCH, WHO LOST THE USE OF HER LEGS AS A RESULT OF AN INJURY SHE SUFFERED IN THE ARMY, IS A WORLD-CLASS SWIMMER. AT THE SYDNEY PARALYMPICS IN 2000, KEREN WON THREE GOLD MEDALS: THE 100-METER BACKSTROKE (1:18:60), THE 100-METER FREESTYLE (1:10:25), AND THE 50-METER FREESTYLE (31:85).

- GAL FRIEDMAN, WINDSURFER EXTRAORDINAIRE, TOOK THE BRONZE MEDAL AT THE 1996 ATLANTA OLYMPICS IN THE MEN'S MISTRAL (BOARD) COMPETITION.

◆ *Get a JNF tzedakah box and make a weekly practice of dropping a coin in it.* Other members of your household should be encouraged to do the same. Not only will you all develop the habit of giving tzedakah, but you will also feel a growing connection to the Land of Israel.

◆ *Celebrate special events (birthdays, anniversaries, graduations) by planting a tree in Israel.* The JNF will send a beautiful certificate in honor of the occasion. You can also plant a tree in memory of a loved one.

6

Spend a summer in Israel. Israel is a beautiful country. Its climate varies from the chill of the snow-capped Mount Hermon in the north to the sunny beaches of Eilat in the far south. There are archaeological remains of biblical Israel, sports arenas, museums, concert halls, and shopping malls with cineplexes, food courts, and the latest fashions. You can ice-skate in the desert and swim with the dolphins, surf the Net or the ocean, and visit a biblical zoo and a camel clinic. But Israel is more than an exciting and fun tour. It is *the* Jewish country. Those who have never been to Israel are in for a surprise. Jews do everything—they drive the buses, walk the beat as police officers, are construction workers, professors, film stars, and politicians. In Israel, banks and schools close on Saturday because it is Shabbat, and Jewish holy days are the national holidays, in contrast to Christmas and Easter in Europe and North America.

To learn about teen trips to Israel, talk to your rabbi or youth group leader, or contact your local Jewish federation.

▲ When you visit Israel, you can go to the Western Wall, a supporting wall of the Second Temple.

5

Open a savings account in an Israeli bank. Israeli banks have branch offices in American cities with large Jewish populations. In North America, those banks are Bank Leumi, Bank Hapoalim, and the Mizrachi Bank. Your account will help support Israel in a concrete way.

▶ Israeli street signs are in Hebrew, Arabic, and English.

▲ JNF tzedakah box

8 Donate money. Israel is a worthy cause. Jews have always accepted shared responsibility for the community, with one Jew providing for others in times of need. Helping Jews live in freedom and security in our homeland and as productive members of the international community is an ideal that you can help realize.

The leading means of getting donations from here to there is the United Jewish Appeal, which exists in almost every community in North America. An alternative organization to which you can contribute tzedakah is the New Israel Fund, which channels money to organizations that develop Jewish-Arab relations, encourage religious pluralism, and improve the status of women in Israel. Yet another organization that channels American contributions to many deserving Israeli institutions is poet Danny Siegel's Ziv Tzedakah Fund.

7 Correspond with an Israeli teen. Using e-mail, "snail mail," or fax, get to know an Israeli teen firsthand. Compare notes on what it's like growing up here and in Israel. Ask your principal or rabbi for suggestions on how to find a pen pal.

▲ These teens are members of the tzofim, the Israeli scouts.

One way to lend money to the Israeli government is by purchasing Israeli bonds. Getting gift money? How about using part of it to buy an Israeli bond?

Finally, you can contribute to your religious denomination's fund-raising efforts for its synagogues and religious schools in Israel.

▶ **When you buy Israeli bonds, you are investing in the Jewish future and supporting the Jewish homeland.**

Self-Portrait

⭐ THE BEST GIFT I EVER RECEIVED WAS _____ I VALUED IT BECAUSE

_____ THE BEST GIFT I EVER GAVE WAS _____

WHAT MADE IT SPECIAL WAS _____

⭐ I THINK THE BEST OCCASIONS FOR GIVING A GIFT OF AN ISRAELI BOND OR A TREE PLANTED

IN ISRAEL ARE:

___ JEWISH HOLIDAYS AND   ___ BIRTHDAYS   ___ GRADUATIONS   ___ TO THANK SOMEONE
LIFE-CYCLE EVENTS

OTHER _____

WHAT MAKES SUCH A GIFT SPECIAL IS _____

⭐ HOW DO YOU THINK A NON-JEWISH FRIEND OF YOURS WOULD RESPOND TO A GIFT OF A TREE

PLANTED IN ISRAEL FOR A BIRTHDAY? AS A GESTURE OF THANKS? _____

_____

To deepen my commitment to the mitzvah of *ahavat Tziyon*, I chose to _____

_____

because _____

_____

This is what I did (provide a detailed description): _____

_____

_____

_____

I would/wouldn't choose to do it again because _____

_____

I have/have not been to Israel. This influences my feelings toward Israel in the following

ways _____

_____

_____

I think it is/isn't important for all Jews to visit Israel because _____

_____

_____

_____

My other thoughts on observing this mitzvah: _____

_____

_____

_____

_____

⑦ Bal Tashhit

every day is earth day

The earth is Adonai's, with all it contains; the world and all its inhabitants.

—Psalm 24:1

April showers are a blessing. The cool water fills the earth's lakes and oceans, cleans and refreshes our bodies, and helps fields and gardens grow. Because we use water every day, we sometimes take it for granted. But water is a precious gift, like the air we breathe and the trees from which we seek shade, gather fruits, make paper, and carve furniture.

For which of nature's other gifts are you especially grateful in your daily life? What would our daily lives be like without them? How many of these gifts are necessary for us to live, and how many simply make our lives more convenient or pleasurable?

We Are Caretakers

The Torah begins with a challenge. After creating the world, God instructs the first humans to "replenish the earth and master it" *(Genesis 1:28)*. As the caretakers of the Garden of Eden, they are to "till it and tend it" *(Genesis 2:15)*. The beginning of the Torah thus reminds us that we live in a world we did not create, a world we do not own; we are the tenants of God's world. As such, it is our role to live responsibly and respectfully as a part of Creation. We demonstrate our mastery of the earth by using our talents to enrich and sustain all life, not by wasting its resources or endangering other creatures.

Conservation Is an Ancient Jewish Tradition

The mitzvah of *bal tashḥit,* which means "do not destroy," requires us to think about how we live in relationship to the earth, how we can live successfully and happily while limiting our extravagance and wastefulness, and how we can restore a balance between our need to live off the earth and our need to preserve its resources for tomorrow, next year, and the generations to come. In short, *bal tashḥit* prohibits us from being wasteful. It reminds us that the objects we make and own are not so much created by us as borrowed from nature.

Too often, we disregard our ancient tradition of conserving the natural world, treating the earth as if we were its masters instead of its caretakers. The effects of the overproduction of "stuff"—cars, computers, TVs, product packaging, plastic shopping bags, disposable eating utensils, etc.—together with our constant need for convenience, have global implications that have already caused permanent damage to the natural order.

We have the knowledge to prevent this destruction. The question is: Do we have the vision and the will to change the way we live?

▲ The talent, creativity, and intelligence that transform a tree trunk into a harp reflect the human ability to borrow from nature to add to the beauty of Creation.

Self-Portrait

⭐ **MY FAVORITE SEASON OF THE YEAR IS** _____

BECAUSE _____

_____

⭐ **IF I WERE TO PLANT A GARDEN, I WOULD FILL IT WITH**

_____

⭐ **IF I COULD EAT ONLY FRUITS AND VEGETABLES, I WOULD CHOOSE TO EAT:**

_____

_____

_____

⭐ **MY FAVORITE OUTDOOR SPORTS ARE** _____

_____

_____

it's a TRaDitioN

It is a Jewish tradition to recite one hundred blessings each day. One way to meet that goal and to remember your responsibility to help care for the wonders of Creation is to recite a blessing each time you see, taste, hear, or smell one of life's natural wonders. Here are a few examples of such blessings, called *birchot hanehenin*, or "blessings of enjoyment."

Blessing said as you enjoy a sunrise, a majestic mountain, or a shooting star:

בָּרוּךְ אַתָּה יְיָ אֱלֹהֵינוּ מֶלֶךְ הָעוֹלָם,
עֹשֶׂה מַעֲשֵׂה בְרֵאשִׁית.

Blessed are You, Adonai our God, Sovereign of the universe, the Source of Creation.

Blessing said as you inhale the sweet fragrance of flowers in bloom:

בָּרוּךְ אַתָּה יְיָ אֱלֹהֵינוּ מֶלֶךְ הָעוֹלָם,
בּוֹרֵא עִשְׂבֵי בְשָׂמִים.

Blessed are You, Adonai our God, Sovereign of the universe, who creates fragrant plants.

Blessing said as you see a rainbow arching against the sky:

בָּרוּךְ אַתָּה יְיָ אֱלֹהֵינוּ מֶלֶךְ הָעוֹלָם,
זוֹכֵר הַבְּרִית, וְנֶאֱמָן בִּבְרִיתוֹ,
וְקַיָּם בְּמַאֲמָרוֹ.

Blessed are You, Adonai our God, Sovereign of the universe, who remembers the covenant, is faithful to it, and keeps Your promise.

To which covenant does the third blessing refer? The Bible tells how after the Flood, God established a covenant with Noah, his descendants, and all living creatures to never again bring a flood to destroy the earth. God placed a rainbow in the sky as a sign of this covenant. You may want to make a poster of a rainbow to hang in your bedroom as a reminder to observe the mitzvah of *bal tashhit*.

Take a moment to think about an aspect of nature that you particularly value and want to protect. Write a blessing of thanksgiving for this gift of nature.

_____

_____

_____

▲ Imagine what the world would be like if there were no flowers, or if flowers had no fragrance or color. When you think about such possibilities, you may develop a greater appreciation of the wonder of Creation.

think about it!

HOW DOES *bal tashhit* FIT INTO YOUR SENSE OF WHO YOU ARE AND OF THE ADULT YOU WANT TO BECOME?

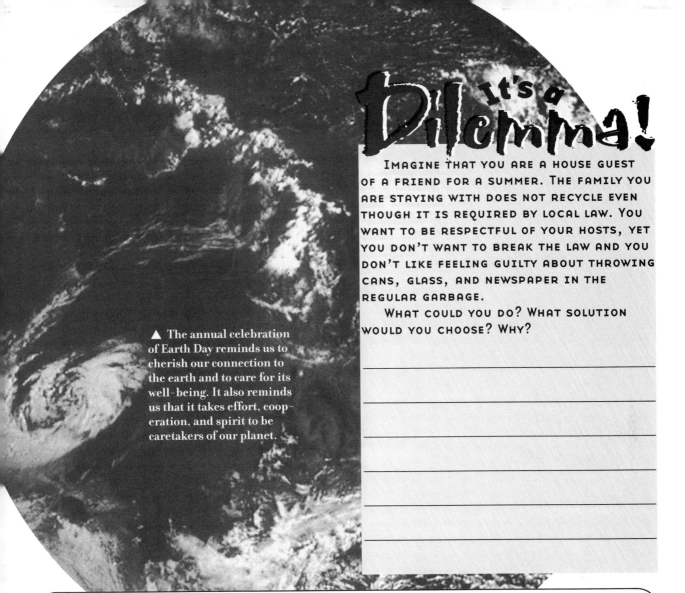

▲ The annual celebration of Earth Day reminds us to cherish our connection to the earth and to care for its well-being. It also reminds us that it takes effort, cooperation, and spirit to be caretakers of our planet.

It's a Dilemma!

IMAGINE THAT YOU ARE A HOUSE GUEST OF A FRIEND FOR A SUMMER. THE FAMILY YOU ARE STAYING WITH DOES NOT RECYCLE EVEN THOUGH IT IS REQUIRED BY LOCAL LAW. YOU WANT TO BE RESPECTFUL OF YOUR HOSTS, YET YOU DON'T WANT TO BREAK THE LAW AND YOU DON'T LIKE FEELING GUILTY ABOUT THROWING CANS, GLASS, AND NEWSPAPER IN THE REGULAR GARBAGE.

WHAT COULD YOU DO? WHAT SOLUTION WOULD YOU CHOOSE? WHY?

_____

_____

_____

_____

_____

_____

_____

Planet Earth Is Our Everyday Concern

There is a little-known Jewish ritual that is performed every twenty-eight years: *birkat haḥammah*, meaning "blessing the sun." According to the Talmud, the vernal equinox cycle takes twenty-eight years. It is a tradition for Jews to thank God for the sun and its life-giving rays at the beginning of each new solar cycle. This is one of many Jewish rituals designed to sensitize us to the wonder of nature.

As the year of the *birkat haḥammah* approaches, a flurry of articles are written and classes are held to educate Jews about this ritual. But once the date has passed, the excitement wears off, and most of us forget that such an event ever happened.

Many countries hold an annual celebration known as Earth Day. Like the Jewish ritual of *birkat haḥammah*, it directs our attention to the importance of the natural world. And as with *birkat haḥammah*, the hoopla and commitment that surround Earth Day reach a crescendo and are soon forgotten.

However, although the years in which we perform the ritual of *birkat haḥammah* come and go, and although Earth Day passes, the earth itself remains. This planet is our home. It requires our attention not every twenty-eight years or once a year, but every day.

What do you do on a daily basis that shows concern for our planet? What could you or others do more (or less) of to make a difference and help save our planet?

How we use resources in our homes and personal lives can have a significant impact on the health of our planet. The following actions can make a difference.

Ready! Set! Go!

Contact an environmental group.

There are many groups that can help you learn more about the environment and gain a deeper appreciation of nature. There are foundations that raise funds to purchase wild lands; organizations that sponsor camping and hiking expeditions; and groups that lobby politicians on behalf of environmental issues. For information on environmental groups, contact your local library or surf the Net.

A Jewish environmental group, the Coalition on the Environment and Jewish Life (COEJL), has materials for religious school programs, lecture series, and social action, and has produced many publications.

Practice Jewish rituals that reflect our tradition of connectedness to nature.

The Jewish way of life encourages our appreciation of Creation and our partnership with God.

◆ *Recite* birchot hanehenin, *or "blessings of enjoyment," such as the ones on page 62.* These blessings can be found in most traditional prayer books.

◆ *Buy a Jewish calendar and make a point of following it throughout the seasons.* The Jewish calendar corresponds to natural phenomena: the length of the year is determined by the cycle of the sun, and the months are determined by the cycle of the moon. By living according to the Jewish calendar, you can become more connected to the rhythms of nature.

▼ "The Creator of heaven, who alone is God, who formed the earth and made it...did not establish it as waste, but formed it for habitation" (Isaiah 45:18).

Notice when Rosh Ḥodesh (the "new month") begins and correlate that date with the phase of the moon. When the moon is not visible or when it is just a sliver, then it is Rosh Ḥodesh. When the full moon is visible, around the fifteenth day of the Jewish month, then the month is half over.

◆ *Celebrate Tu B'Shevat.* While almost every Jewish holy day and festival reflects some aspect of how we should live in harmony with the earth, one day is unique in its celebration of trees—Tu B'Shevat, the fifteenth day of the month of Shevat, the New Year of the Trees. Increasingly, this holiday is being celebrated with a Tu B'Shevat seder. The themes of the meal include appreciating the beauty of the world, the cycle of the seasons, and our special love for the Land of Israel. Often the evening concludes with the planting of a tree. If you would like to conduct a Tu B'Shevat seder at your religious school, synagogue, or home, ask your principal or rabbi for guidance.

 **Conserve water.** Because there is a limited amount of usable water (only three percent of all the water available on the earth is fresh water), we must make conservation a way of life, not simply a response to an emergency.

Some simple actions can reduce the amount of water we waste or pollute: Turn off the shower head when you lather up, the water tap when you brush your teeth, and the faucet when you soap dirty dishes. Remember, much of what we do is simply habit, and bad habits can be changed to good ones. What at first you may consider an inconvenience, with practice can become a very natural as well as environmentally sound way of life.

▲ Developing the habits of recycling rather than discarding and of bicycling rather than traveling short distances by car are practical and effective ways to show your concern for the environment and your commitment to Jewish values.

 Whenever possible, recycle. The United States recycles only 10 percent of its garbage (in contrast to Japan, which recycles 50 percent). Glass and plastic bottles, metal products, and paper can often be recycled. If your community doesn't already have a recycling program, call your state or local government for information about starting one and then get involved. As a way to improve the world, recycling is an excellent project for a religious school or a youth group.

Avoid using plastics. Styrofoam and other plastic foams are made with chlorofluorocarbons (CFCs), which destroy the ozone layer and don't decompose. When in restaurants that use foam or plastic, ask for paper instead. At home, use mugs instead of paper cups, and always use paper cups instead of plastic if a disposable cup is the only option.

Store food in containers rather than in plastic wrap or aluminum foil. In general, it is a good idea to use something than can be reused rather than something that must be thrown out after one use.

Teens
Make a Difference
Anna Shapiro

Anna Shapiro comes from Raleigh, North Carolina. In high school she was a member of the student council and captain of the varsity track team. She also attended her synagogue's religious school. After studying the tradition of *bal tashḥit*, she decided to turn her knowledge into action. So, she formed a recycling club at her high school.

Anna worked with a local recycling center, raised money, and reached out to friends, members of the school service club, and the student council. At first *everyone* was enthusiastic, but *few* were actually willing to pitch in and do the work of creating recycling containers, placing them around the school, publicizing the campaign, and arranging for the collection of the recyclable materials.

But Anna wasn't discouraged. A few friends came through, so she worked with them as she continued to involve others. By the end of the school year, her recycling club was the biggest and smoothest running student organization in the school.

Anna was awarded her school's Community Service award. Proud of her success, she said, "Believing in yourself is all you need to accomplish anything."☼

◀ **How can you help improve the world?**

Believe in YOURSELF

FEELING DISCOURAGED? OVERWHELMED BY ALL THAT NEEDS TO BE DONE? REMEMBER, LIKE MANY OF THE EARTH'S NATURAL RESOURCES, HOPES AND DREAMS ARE RENEWABLE. IF YOU HAVE AN IDEA OF HOW TO HELP MAKE THE WORLD A BETTER PLACE, BELIEVE IN YOURSELF AND KEEP ON GOING!

YOU DON'T SAY!

"WHOEVER DESTROYS SOMETHING USEFUL IS VIOLATING THE PRINCIPLE, 'YOU SHALL NOT BE DESTRUCTIVE.'"
—*Midrash Aggadah to Judges 20*

HOW CAN YOU REMIND YOURSELF, ON A DAILY BASIS, TO PROTECT AND CARE FOR THE GIFTS OF CREATION?

_____

_____

_____

_____

To deepen my commitment to the mitzvah of *bal tashḥit*, I chose to _____

_____

because _____

_____

This is what I did (provide a detailed description): _____

_____

_____

I would/wouldn't choose to do this again because _____

_____

I can persuade others to observe *bal tashḥit* by _____

_____

I think that observing the mitzvah of *bal tashḥit*, can/cannot help me become the adult I

want to become because _____

_____

_____

My other thoughts on observing this mitzvah: _____

_____

_____

_____

_____

_____

_____

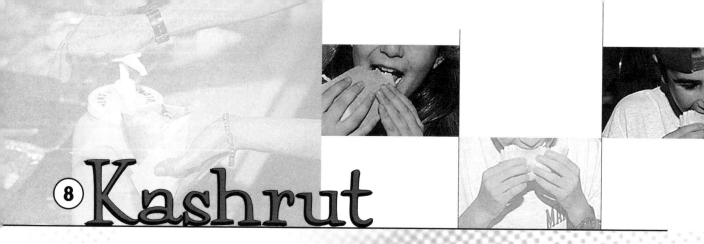

⑧ Kashrut

you are what you eat

> *The purpose [of kashrut] is to refine humanity.*
>
> — *Genesis Rabbah 44:1*

Can you imagine a Jewish celebration that doesn't include food? Can you imagine Rosh Hashanah without honey and apples? Ḥanukkah without golden brown latkes? Purim without fruit-filled hamantashen? Passover without matzah ball soup, rich with parsley and dill? What about Jewish weddings, baby namings, and bar and bat mitzvah celebrations? Can you imagine these celebrations without a generous supply of food?

In our tradition we use food to welcome friends and extend hospitality, to praise God, and to remind ourselves of important events and values. On Passover, we eat maror—bitter herbs—to remind ourselves of the bitterness of oppression; on Ḥanukkah, we eat foods made with oil, such as latkes and *sufganiyot* (fried jelly donuts), in remembrance of the Temple oil that miraculously burned for eight days; and on Tu B'Shevat we eat fruits from Israel—almonds, dates, figs, carob, and pomegranates—to remind us to keep our homeland in bloom and to renew the earth's resources by planting trees.

But the most important tradition—which we are taught to observe even on ordinary days—reminds us that every meal, every snack, every lick and nibble not only can give us pleasure, but also can honor God and add to life's holiness. This tradition is the mitzvah of keeping kosher, *sh'mirat kashrut*.

The Dietary Laws

In the book of Leviticus, after listing the laws of kashrut, God says, "Therefore, become holy, for I am holy" (*Leviticus 11:45*). And so, for more than three thousand years, Judaism has taught us through the laws of kashrut to satisfy our physical need for nourishment in a way that feeds our souls as well. At its core, keeping kosher restrains us from impulsively grabbing and devouring food. Because it links our food choices with the well-being of Creation, it focuses us on the holiness of all life as we gather, prepare,

▲ Apples, honey, and round hallah stuffed with raisins add to the sweet celebration of Rosh Hashanah.

and eat our meals. Observing kashrut reminds us to treat the earth's resources with respect and compassion.

The broad guidelines of kashrut come from the Torah and are detailed in the Talmud. They are divided into three general areas: Separating milk and meat, regulating the slaughter of animals, and prohibiting certain meats.

◆ *Separate milk and meat.* The tradition of separating milk and meat is based on the biblical commandment, "You shall not boil a kid in its mother's milk" (*Exodus 34:26* and *Deuteronomy 14:21*). Some scholars believe this tradition was developed to emphasize the Jewish reverence for life and devotion to the living. Perhaps because milk sustains an infant, it is a symbol of life and nurturance. To eat or cook an animal in the very liquid that nourished it would be a cruel perversion of milk's natural purpose.

The rabbis of the Talmud extended the biblical custom of separation to include waiting between eating meals that contain meat—beef, veal, or fowl—and those that contain dairy, as well as using separate utensils, pots, and plates for meat meals and dairy meals.

◀ Have you ever felt hungry enough to "eat a horse" or a King Kong-size hamburger? At such times, what helps you make good choices?

Self-Portrait

★ MY FAVORITE THREE FOODS ARE: _____

★ MY FAVORITE HOLIDAY MEAL INCLUDES THESE FOODS: _____

_____

★ I PREFER TO EAT ALONE WHEN _____

BECAUSE _____

_____

★ I PREFER TO EAT WITH MY FAMILY WHEN _____

BECAUSE _____

_____

★ I PREFER TO EAT WITH MY FRIENDS WHEN _____

BECAUSE _____

_____

★ I WOULD DESCRIBE MYSELF AS SOMEONE WHO EATS TO LIVE/LIVES TO EAT BECAUSE

_____

_____

★ I HAVE/HAVE NOT FELT A SENSE OF HOLINESS IN RELATIONSHIP TO EATING. (IF YOU HAVE, DESCRIBE THE SITUATION—FOR EXAMPLE, A HOLIDAY CELEBRATION—AND YOUR FEELINGS. IF YOU HAVE NOT, DISCUSS WHY YOU THINK THAT EATING CAN OR CANNOT BE A HOLY ACT.)

_____

_____

_____

- *Observe the laws of ritual slaughter.* In part to increase our awareness of the value and sanctity of animal life, a central law of kashrut is *sheḥitah*, "ritual slaughter." *Sheḥitah* ensures that slaughtering will be done with the least possible pain to the animals. It also includes the requirement to drain the slaughtered animal's blood before its meat can be eaten. The blood (which, like milk, is a symbol of life) is drained from the carcass to remind us that we humans do not own the world or the lives of its inhabitants.
- *Do not eat certain meats.* The laws of kashrut permit us to eat only those animals that fit into certain categories—birds that fly and are not scavengers, mammals that chew their cud and have cloven hooves, and fish that have both fins and scales and are not scavengers. Almost all insects are prohibited. (Some types of grasshoppers are permitted.)

Kashrut and Jewish Identity

Kashrut creates a relationship between the act of eating and God, our identity, our community, and our morality. For thousands of years, our dietary laws have helped unify Jews, solidifying Jewish identity, forging a link with Jews throughout time and across the globe, and strengthening family and friends as communities devoted to a humane order on Earth. Through the laws of kashrut, we learn that we can discipline ourselves, enjoying the pleasures of life while affirming our responsibility to care for God's world.

The commitment to observe kashrut can be a challenge, not unlike the decision to lose weight. Changing your daily diet for the sake of Jewish unity and to nurture a sense of holiness in your life may, at times, even feel like a burden. The key is to take one step at a time so that you can enjoy it. Only by progressing gradually, advancing to a new step when—and only when—you are ready, can you develop a sense of *simḥat mitzvah*, "joy of the commandment," rather than feel that you are simply adding another burden to your life.

▲ Beyond observing the laws of kashrut, how can you show your concern for animals?

▲ Kashrut connects us to Jews around the world. This French butcher shop sells kosher meat as well as a variety of kosher packaged foods. It is like a welcome home sign for Jews visiting from other cities or countries.

◀ How and what we eat reflect our values and our priorities. The popularity of fast food indicates a concern for speed and efficiency. Kashrut reflects a concern for holiness and community.

Ready! Set! GO!

Here are some suggestions that can help enrich your experience of kashrut if you already keep kosher, or that can help you move toward kashrut if you currently do not observe the dietary laws. Whatever your situation, it is important to remember that it is also a mitzvah to be respectful of other Jews—including the members of your family—who may not make the same choices as you.

1 **Recite Hamotzi before eating.** Whether you keep kosher or not, reciting Hamotzi can remind you that we humans are not the owners of the earth and that Judaism connects the physical need to eat with the spiritual need to show reverence for God and for life. For these reasons, you may also want to recite the Birkat Hamazon, or Grace After Meals.

2 **Abstain from all pig products.** Although pork has no greater biblical significance than any other *treif* (non-kosher) food, in later Jewish tradition the pig became the symbol of nonkosher food.

Perhaps because pigs were said to wallow in filth, or because they were popular in Greek and Roman cultures, eating pork became synonymous with abandoning Judaism. As a first step toward keeping kosher, refrain from eating pig products: ham, bacon, pork chops, ribs, sausage, and so forth.

Avoiding pork will help you pay greater attention to what you eat and lead to a public identification with the dietary laws. This can heighten your sense of Jewish identity and solidarity with other Jews.

Protecting a fragile beauty

Pescadero Point is the northern boundary of the Carmel Bay Ecological Reserve. Within the reserve, which extends to Point Lobos south of Carmel, you may not take any marine invertebrates, such as crabs, starfish, abalone, snails, etc.

▲ **Although shellfish are treif, like pigs and other nonkosher animals, they are a sacred part of Creation and we are obligated to be respectful of them and to care for them.**

 **Refrain from eating shellfish.** The Torah mentions the prohibition of all shellfish immediately after the prohibition of pork. Many theories have attempted to explain the shellfish prohibition. (Shellfish are the "vacuum cleaners" of the water world, sucking in the garbage that floats in the sea, or shellfish simply don't share the characteristics of the Bible's "ideal" fish, those with fins and scales.)

Shellfish includes clams, oysters, mussels, abalone, crab, lobster, octopus, squid, sea cucumber, shrimp, prawn, and the like. If you are uncertain about what fits in this category, use the simple biblical standard: If it has scales and fins, it's okay. If not, then skip it.

 **Separate dairy products from meat products**. All dairy products, and any food with dairy ingredients—for example, bread or cake made with cream, butter, or cheese—are considered milk, and anything with a meat base (including poultry) or its byproducts is considered meat. Don't mix the two, whether in cooking or in eating. This means no more cheeseburgers, no cream sauces or butter on meat, no milk or cheese with delicatessen sandwiches, and no meat in cheese lasagna.

 **Observe a minimal waiting period between eating meat and eating a dairy product.** In most North American Jewish communities, the waiting period is three hours after the end of the meat meal. There need not be a waiting period after a dairy meal.

Check the ingredients of food to determine whether it is kosher. Read package labels. This examination can take one of two forms:

♦ *Purchase only food that has a kosher label on it.* A kosher label tells you that the food was produced or prepared under the supervision of a specific rabbinic authority.

▲ Look for one of these symbols of kashrut on food labels.

♦ *Purchase foods without a rabbinic certification only after checking that the ingredients are not treif.* For example, be careful to check for lard (pig fat), which is found in many baking mixes and pie crusts. If a label doesn't specify that a shortening is 100 percent vegetable shortening, then assume it is not kosher. Also, note that if a product is made with casein or sodium caseinate, it is dairy.

Eat only "biblically permitted" meat. This is the next step in observing a higher standard of kashrut. The only animals that can be used for kosher slaughter are noncarnivorous domestic poultry (such as chicken, turkey, duck, capon, and goose) and land mammals that have cloven hooves and chew their cud. Cattle, deer, goats, and sheep are permitted. Rabbit and swine are not (rabbits don't have hooves, and pigs don't chew their cud). If possible, eat only meat that has been bought from a kosher butcher.

▲ All these foods are kosher and can be found in most supermarkets.

Don't Be Shy

Sometimes we are shy or embarrassed about expressing our religious needs. For instance, some people find that having to tell a host or hostess that they no longer eat nonkosher foods, or mix meat and milk, presents a stumbling block in the path of keeping kosher. But imagine inviting a Hindu friend over for a meal. Wouldn't you want to serve something your guest could eat? Wouldn't you appreciate being told that observant Hindus don't eat meat? Similarly, imagine hosting a diabetic or someone with food allergies. You certainly would want to accommodate such people.

Jews can expect that same concern and support from others. So, when invited out, speak up, and when hosting, be sure to ask whether your guests have dietary restrictions or preferences.

think about it!

Some people consider veal *treif* because of the cruelty with which many calves are raised. For example, calves often nurse for only a day or two before they are removed from their mothers' care and put in slotted stalls without space to move or lie down. People who view veal as *treif* do so as a modern interpretation of the laws of kashrut. They believe that eating animals that have been forced to live under abusive conditions violates the compassionate values of kashrut. What do you think?

YOU DON'T SAY!

"There will be no end of wars in the world until people stop killing animals. Slaughter and justice cannot dwell together."
–Isaac Bashevis Singer

Do you think that being a vegetarian is a practical way to pursue justice and peace? Why or why not?

_____

_____

_____

Reach Out to the Community

We cannot be Jewish alone—we need the community. So, don't keep kosher alone! There is no need to become isolated. Reach out to people, perhaps from your synagogue, who can provide guidance and tips from their personal experience. Speak to your rabbi about practical concerns and about how you can address differences that may exist between the choices you want to make and those of your family.

"Neutral Foods"

Poultry—chicken, turkey, duck, and Cornish game hen—is considered meat. Fish, however, is parve (neither meat nor milk) and may be served with both dairy meals and with meat meals. Mayonnaise (without milk additives), mustard, and ketchup are also parve, as are eggs, fruit, grains, and vegetables. While some margarine is parve, most is dairy. The "kosher" label, if there is one, will indicate if the contents are parve or dairy.

Note: The government standard for identifying a product as dairy or nondairy is different than the kashrut standard. When in doubt—for example, when considering nondairy creamers—look for a kosher label to check the details.

THE WISDOM OF MODERATION

The ultimate ideal of Judaism is a state of harmony between all living things—a world of vegetarians. All vegetables and fruit are naturally kosher (literally, "fit" or "proper"). In fact, the Torah portrays Adam and Eve as vegetarians in the Garden of Eden. But insisting on an absolute ideal often results in its opposite. Rather than imposing unattainable ideals, the mitzvot channel human urges into manageable and constructive forms. Kashrut is Judaism's brilliant compromise, instilling a concern for the humane treatment of animals without denying the human desire for meat.

It's a Dilemma!

You're hanging out with some kids at a friend's house. The group decides to order in a couple of pizzas. Based on your experience, you know that the general preference is for sausage and pepperoni. You have recently committed yourself to not eating pork products and to not mixing meat with milk. What do you do? Do you wait to find out what your friends want to order? Do you announce beforehand that you don't want meat on your pizza? Do you talk about your recent commitment to kashrut? Do you not say anything?

_____

_____

Does it matter if your friends are Jewish or not? Why?

_____

_____

_____

Explain why you think your solution is the best response to the situation.

_____

_____

_____

Eat only kosher varieties of fish. The general guideline is the requirement of fins and scales. This excludes bullfish, eels, gars, lampreys, monkfish, puffers, sharks, rays, skates, triggerfish, and wolffish. In addition, fish that are scavengers are generally considered nonkosher as well. This means no catfish. Most rabbis consider swordfish and sturgeon to be kosher, although some Orthodox rabbis do not.

Eat meat only from a kosher butcher. Limit your consumption of meat to kosher animals that have been slaughtered and prepared according to the laws of kashrut. Speak to your rabbi if you need additional guidance.

Become a vegetarian. The Talmud instructs us that our first choice should be vegetarian foods, that we need "not eat meat unless [we] have a craving for it." You may want to become a vegetarian in observance of the mitzvot of caring for your health (sh'mirat habriyut) and

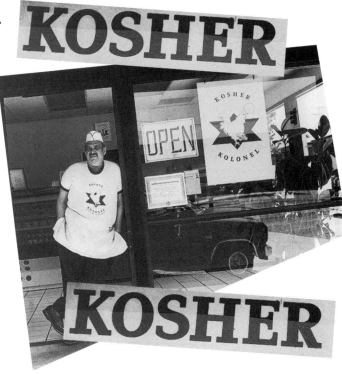

▲ Cities with large Jewish populations often have kosher restaurants, butchers, and groceries that serve a variety of popular and gourmet foods.

compassion for animals (tza'ar ba'alei ḥayyim), as well as in the spirit of kashrut's reverence for life. (The Nobel Prize-winning author Isaac Bashevis Singer was once asked if he was a vegetarian for health reasons. He answered, "Yes, for the chicken's health.")

◀ A vegetarian diet can be tasty as well as easy to cater to when you eat out.

To deepen my commitment to the mitzvah of observing kashrut, I chose to _____

_____

because _____

_____

This is what I did (provide a detailed description): _____

_____

_____

I would/wouldn't choose to do this again because _____

_____

I think that keeping kosher is/isn't a meaningful way to show respect for the holiness of

life because _____

_____

_____

What I learned about myself by observing this mitzvah is _____

_____

_____

My other thoughts on observing this mitzvah: _____

_____

_____

_____

_____

_____

_____

Sh'mirat Habriyut

be your best friend

By keeping the body in health and strength one walks in the ways of God....[Therefore] it is a person's duty to avoid whatever is harmful to the body and to cultivate habits that lead to good health.

— *Maimonides*

According to legend, one day, as the great sage Hillel was leaving class, a student asked, "Where are you going?"

"To the bathhouse to perform a religious duty, a mitzvah," Hillel answered.

"What religious duty could possibly be fulfilled there?" asked the young man in surprise.

"Bathing, of course," replied Hillel.

"I don't understand," said the student. "Why is bathing a religious duty?"

"As you know," Hillel responded, "cleaning statues that are created in the image of the king is considered an important and distinguished responsibility. How much greater, then, is the obligation to care for the human body, which is created in *God's* image."

Caring for Ourselves Is a Religious Duty

Just as our tradition teaches us that all human beings are created in God's image, it also instructs us that all human life is sacred. Therefore, it is a religious duty—a mitzvah—not only to treat others well but also to treat ourselves with care and respect, physically and mentally.

Sh'mirat habriyut, caring for one's health, is a modern interpretation of Judaism's traditional concern that we treat our bodies with respect. It includes developing good health habits, such as eating nutritious food and exercising regularly; establishing nurturing relationships with friends and family; developing self-esteem; and learning to handle stress.

▲ Human beings do not roll off an assembly line like mannequins. We are each different. Learning who you are and what works for you, what you need and what you want, is an important part of becoming an adult.

think about it!

THE TORAH TELLS THE STORY OF HOW GOD CREATED THE FIRST PERSON—ADAM—FROM DUST AND THEN BLEW THE BREATH OF LIFE, A *neshamah*, INTO HIM. THUS, OUR TRADITION TEACHES THAT SINCE CREATION EVERY PERSON RECEIVES AT BIRTH A *neshamah*, A PERSONAL CONNECTION WITH GOD, A DIVINE SPARK OF HOLINESS THAT GLOWS INSIDE THE BODY.

THE ANCIENT JEWISH PHILOSOPHER, PHILO OF ALEXANDRIA, WHOSE WRITINGS FOCUS ON BIBLICAL STORIES, TAUGHT, "THE BODY IS THE SOUL'S HOUSE. SHOULDN'T WE THEREFORE TAKE CARE OF OUR HOUSE SO THAT IT DOESN'T FALL TO RUIN?"

WHAT DO HILLEL AND PHILO'S TEACHINGS HAVE IN COMMON? DO YOU SHARE THEIR POINT OF VIEW, OR HAVE YOU A DIFFERENT ONE? WHY?

MY CHANGING PALETTE

What colors describe your different moods?

1. When I'm happy, color me _____

2. When I'm angry, color me _____

3. When I'm worried, color me _____

4. When I'm sad, color me _____

5. When I'm proud, color me _____

Self-Portrait

Your teen years can be filled with many new adventures and pleasures, such as a first love and a driver's license. But they also may include increased pressures, often exerted by friends and other peers, that can affect your ability to be true to yourself, to think independently, and to be who you are.

One way to resist negative peer pressure is to know what you believe in and care about. Below, list ten values and beliefs you have that can be your personal "Ten Commandments"—that can help you care for and be true to yourself.

1. I believe _____

2. I believe _____

3. I believe _____

4. I believe _____

5. I believe _____

6. I believe _____

7. I believe _____

8. I believe _____

9. I believe _____

10. I believe _____

One example of how positive peer pressure has helped me is: _____

_____

One way in which my friends help me make decisions that are right for me is:

_____

Sh'mirat habriyut also requires that you get to know your-self—how much food, rest, and exercise you need to feel your best; how you react to new, unexpected, and unfamiliar situations; and what your stress buttons are. For example, how might you react to the increased tension and excitement of attending a new school, or auditioning for a school play, or trying out for a sports team? Do you think it would affect your mood? your eating or sleeping habits? your personal relationships? By knowing your physical and emotional needs and your coping style, you can make better decisions about how to care for yourself, and about when, how, and who to reach out to for help.

 # Know Yourself!

THINK ABOUT THE RELATIONSHIP BETWEEN YOUR MOODS AND YOUR ABILITY TO CARE FOR YOURSELF. WHEN YOU ARE ANXIOUS OR UPSET, DO YOU REACH OUT TO OTHERS AND NURTURE YOURSELF WITH HEALTHY AMOUNTS OF FOOD AND EXERCISE, OR DO YOU WITHDRAW AND DEPRIVE YOUR BODY OF THE SUPPORT AND CARE IT NEEDS TO REMAIN HEALTHY? HOW DO YOU STAY FOCUSED WHEN YOU ARE UNDER PRESSURE, OR GET BACK ON TRACK WHEN YOU HAVE BEEN DERAILED BY A DIFFICULT OR UPSET-TING EXPERIENCE? WHAT WORKS FOR YOU— A HIGHLY STRUCTURED ROUTINE OR A MORE FREEWHEELING STYLE? HOW CAN KNOWING YOURSELF, YOUR LIKES AND DISLIKES, YOUR VALUES AND YOUR TENSION BUTTONS—HELP YOU CARE FOR YOURSELF?

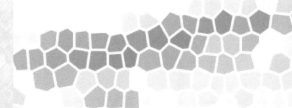

▲ Water sports are favorite summertime activities. But if, on a dare or in the name of fun, we disregard safety rules, we may put ourselves and others in jeopardy. What might you say to someone who is pressuring you to engage in a high-risk behavior?

Jewish Observance Helps Preserve Human Life

Many mitzvot help us live healthy lives and contribute to our self-respect. For example, resting on Shabbat renews us physically and mentally. Maintaining *sh'lom bayit*, family peace, can give us a sense of calm and well-being. Riding a bike (rather than a car) to school in observance of *bal tashḥit* can provide the added plus of reducing our stress and strengthening our muscles. Eating kosher foods and celebrating Sukkot and Shavuot with newly harvested grains and produce affirm the sacred bond between what we eat and what we value. And praying and working with our community can provide us with the emotional support of caring people.

Sh'mirat habriyut is a reminder that Jewish observance is not only what goes on in religious school and in synagogue, on holidays and at life-cycle events, but also what happens at summer camp and in our homes, on vacation and during finals—every day of the week, from Sunday through Shabbat. *Sh'mirat habriyut* is a reminder that Jewish observance involves not only respect for holidays and for other people, but also respect for ourselves— our bodies and our feelings. *Sh'mirat habriyut* can make us stronger, healthier, and happier. And although observing this mitzvah is not an insurance policy against illness or disease, it can help us cope better and live more rewarding and productive lives.

YOU DON'T SAY!

"FRIENDSHIP WITH ONESELF IS ALL-IMPORTANT, BECAUSE WITHOUT IT ONE CANNOT BE FRIENDS WITH ANYONE ELSE."
—*Eleanor Roosevelt*

WHAT DO YOU DO TO BE A GOOD FRIEND TO YOURSELF?

_____

_____

_____

◀ Making Kiddush, a ritual in which modest amounts of wine are drunk, can remind us that even sacred acts become profane if done in excess.

Our sages taught that God makes every person different. Each of us is "one of a kind." This means that no one like you ever lived before. You have something unique to share with others, your own capacity to add holiness to the world. Learn to take good care of yourself. For who you are and what you can contribute are precious.

Ready! Set! Go!

1 **Appreciate the person you are.** Be aware of your strengths and value the special qualities that make you YOU. Perhaps it is your smile and your quirky sense of humor, your energy and generosity, your willingness to help others and to listen when friends need a patient ear, or your unflagging loyalty and kindness that make you the unique person you are.

When you become aware of a shortcoming, be patient with yourself. Remember, no one is perfect. Make the willingness to improve yourself one of your strengths. If you have a serious concern about yourself, consider talking about it with an understanding adult whom you trust.

2 **Create balance in your life.** Sometimes, it is tempting to behave in extreme ways. On Thanksgiving we may overeat, then plunk down to watch football like couch potatoes; on birthdays we may overindulge by staying out late and ignoring our usual responsibilities; and during finals week, we may survive on four hours of sleep and overdrive. But if extreme behavior provides short-term satisfactions and rewards, it is balance that helps us achieve our long-term goals. For example, regular and diverse physical exercise, together with a balanced diet that includes a variety of fruits, vegetables, grains,

▲ Now is a good time to explore your talents and interests. You might participate more actively in sports, take up ceramics or painting, join your synagogue or school choir, or join a science club.

and proteins, as well as a modest amount of unsaturated fat, can more effectively help someone develop *and* maintain an attractive body than diet pills, crash diets, and cigarettes, all of which can do long-term damage.

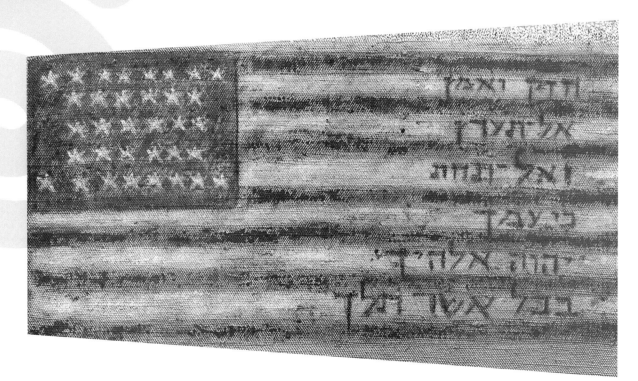

For two weeks, keep a journal of the times when your behavior becomes extreme—when you are argumentative, impatient, or rude; obsessed over or not taking care of your personal hygiene and physical appearance; overeating or starving yourself; exercising compulsively or not at all; sleeping too much or too little; or using alcohol or other drugs. Note what causes your extreme behavior and how you feel at the time—angry, sad, tired, excited, rejected, nervous, proud, happy—and describe the relationship between your feelings and your behavior.

▲ The Hebrew verse on this Union flag from the American Civil War says: "Be strong and have courage, do not be terrified or dismayed, for Adonai, your God, is with you wherever you go" (Joshua 1:9). As these words comforted others in difficult times so, too, may they comfort you.

Then, list two alternative, more balanced ways to handle similar situations. For example, you might write: "When I am intensely happy or nervous, I eat and exercise compulsively. In the future, when I feel overwhelmed by my emotions, instead of reaching for food, I will recite a prayer or affirmation, or take a few deep breaths and listen to some mellow music to help calm myself. I will also limit the time I exercise."

◀ We live in a society that often emphasizes how we look rather than who we are. How do you create a healthy balance? How do you take care of yourself by nurturing both your inner and your outer self?

 **Develop personal guidelines for how you want to treat yourself.** Think about what your values are, what Jewish tradition teaches, and what kind of adult you want to become. Then, refer to—and, if necessary, revise—the "Ten Commandments" you created on page 80. You may want to work on the list with family members and see if everyone can strengthen their commitment to *sh'mirat habriyut.*

4 **Avoid tobacco.** Smoking cigarettes, chewing tobacco, or breathing secondhand smoke all can damage a person's health. In the most serious cases, tobacco use can cause respiratory illness and cancer. But even in less severe instances, it can damage one's lungs to the point where physical activities, such as running, playing tennis, biking, and dancing, become difficult if not impossible.

▲ Sometimes you may become aware of danger because there are brightly colored warning signs posted, for example, on a highway or at the seaside. But more often, only by paying careful attention to what is going on around you will you spot less obvious warning signs, such as illegal drugs at a party or a friend who has become withdrawn and aloof. What invisible warning signs have caught your attention? How have you responded to them?

▲ What are the qualities you look for in a friend? What qualities do you seek to have as a friend?

In addition, nicotine, which is found in tobacco, is habit forming. Ironically, just at the age when we want greater *independence*, many teens become *dependent* on nicotine; and just when social acceptance seems more important than ever, many pick up the nicotine habit, which gives them bad breath and yellow teeth, and makes them look less cool than ever.

If you have never smoked, don't start. If you do smoke, ask for help from your family, your doctor, your school guidance counselor, or the American Cancer Society. And if your friends smoke, either find new friends or excuse yourself and leave when they light up.

5 **Avoid alcohol and other drugs.** Just as smoking cigarettes causes health problems and dependency, so alcohol and illegal drugs, such as marijuana and cocaine, can do physical damage and be habit forming. In addition, they often are used to mask other problems—feelings of alienation, depression, insecurity, or anger. In time, substance abuse complicates rather than cures these problems.

No one is immune from the temptation to participate in high-risk behavior. To help you avoid such risks, make a contract with yourself, your parents, or a good friend. Commit to remaining drug-free. Renew the contract every six months, or every year on your birthday or on Rosh Hashanah. Include a commitment to being alcohol-free.

In your contract, you might also pledge to never get in a car with a driver who has been drinking or who has taken drugs and to make your best effort to discourage such persons from getting behind the wheel. In this way you are protecting not only your life and that of the driver, but also the lives of innocent people who may be on the road. Talk with your parents about the options you have should you find yourself without a ride home, and contact Students Against Drunk Driving (SADD) for more tips and support.

▲ Sometimes it is healing to spend time by yourself when you are upset or blue, and sometimes it is good to discuss your problems with others. To whom do you turn when you need comfort and support?

"IT'S NOT EASY BEING GREEN."
—*Kermit the Frog*

DESCRIBE AN INSTANCE WHEN YOU WERE TRUE TO YOURSELF, DESPITE NEGATIVE PEER PRESSURE, AND DID WHAT YOU BELIEVED WAS RIGHT FOR YOU.

_____

_____

_____

_____

_____

HOW CAN THAT EXPERIENCE INCREASE YOUR DETERMINATION TO RESIST NEGATIVE PEER PRESSURE TO ENGAGE IN HIGH-RISK BEHAVIOR?

_____

_____

_____

It's a Dilemma!

A NEW FRIEND INVITES YOU TO A PARTY AT HER HOME. YOU SHOW UP FASHIONABLY LATE, PSYCHED FOR A GREAT TIME. BUT YOU SOON REALIZE THAT THERE ARE NO ADULTS PRESENT AND THE PARTY IS GETTING OUT OF HAND. NEIGHBORS ARE COMPLAINING THAT THE MUSIC IS TOO LOUD, SOME KIDS HAVE BROUGHT HARD LIQUOR WITH THEM, A SMALL GROUP IS USING DRUGS, AND COUPLES ARE STARTING TO WANDER OFF TOWARD THE BEDROOMS.

HOW CAN YOU TAKE CARE OF YOURSELF IN THIS CIRCUMSTANCE? HOW CAN YOU RESPOND TO NEGATIVE PEER PRESSURE?

_____

_____

_____

_____

_____

_____

_____

A Timeless Internet

Throughout the ages, Jews have kept in touch with past and future generations by studying the teachings of the Bible and the sages, and by adding their own wisdom. Discuss the following teachings with a classmate, friend, or your family, and then contribute your wisdom in the space below.

- "Do not give yourself over to sorrow or distress yourself deliberately....Envy and anger shorten one's life, and anxiety brings premature old age." —*Ben Sira (200 BCE)*
- "If you are in pain, go to a physician!" —*The Talmud*
- "Do not take drugs because they demand periodic doses and your heart will crave them." —*Rabbi Samuel ben Meir (1085—1158 CE)*

_____

_____

_____

An Affirmation

To develop a deeper appreciation of yourself, you may want to recite the following verse as an affirmation when you wake up each morning: "I will praise You, God, for I am awesomely and wondrously made. Marvelous are Your works; my soul knows it well" (*Psalms 139:14*).

YOU DON'T SAY!

BEFORE HE DIED, RABBI ZUSYA SAID TO HIS STUDENTS, "IN THE WORLD TO COME I WILL NOT BE ASKED, 'WHY WEREN'T YOU MOSES?' I WILL BE ASKED, 'WHY WEREN'T YOU ZUSYA?'"

WHAT DO YOU THINK ZUSYA WANTED TO TEACH HIS STUDENTS?

_____

_____

_____

DESCRIBE TWO STRENGTHS THAT HELP MAKE YOU YOU.

_____

_____

_____

HOW DO YOU BUILD ON THESE STRENGTHS TO BECOME THE BEST YOU YOU CAN BE?

_____

_____

_____

_____

_____

WHAT ELSE CAN YOU DO IN ORDER TO BECOME THE BEST YOU?

_____

_____

_____

_____

_____

To deepen my commitment to the mitzvah of *sh'mirat habriyut*, I chose to _____

_____

because _____

_____

This is what I did (provide a detailed description): _____

_____

_____

_____

I would/wouldn't choose to do this again because_____

_____

One way I can improve my physical health is to_____

_____

One way I can better care for my emotional health is to _____

_____

My other thoughts on observing this mitzvah: _____

_____

_____

_____

_____

_____

_____

_____

⑩ Bikkur Holim

reach out and touch someone

The Holy Blessed One visited the sick, as it is written, "Adonai appeared to [Abraham] by the terebinths of Mamre," and so you must also visit the sick.

—Talmud, Sotah

Anyone who has ever been sick knows how important the care and concern of others are. Perhaps you remember the time someone cheered and comforted you, brought a gift that delighted you, e-mailed a list of jokes that made you laugh, or phoned just at the moment you were feeling your lowest. To lift someone's spirits, even with such simple gestures as sending a card or visiting, is truly to make ourselves partners with God.

Offering Comfort and Hope

By sitting with a bedridden friend, we convey that he or she is not forgotten, that the outside world cares. By chatting about plans for the future we offer companionship and hope. By sharing the latest news from school and the most recent adventures of friends, or by talking about the latest movie or rock group, we bring relief from boredom and pain. Most important, perhaps, we help the person maintain his or her connection with the larger world.

Yet even as we recognize the importance of *bikkur holim*—visiting the sick—even as we feel grateful to those loving people who came to visit us when we were ill, we may feel hesitant, awkward, or even fearful when it comes to visiting others.

"A MERRY HEART IS A GOOD MEDICINE."
—*Proverbs 17:22*

HOW CAN THIS SAYING GUIDE YOU WHEN YOU ARE SICK? _____

_____

HOW CAN IT GUIDE YOU WHEN YOU VISIT SOMEONE ELSE WHO IS ILL?

_____

_____

think about it!

THE TALMUD SAYS, "ONE WHO VISITS THE SICK CAUSES THEM TO LIVE." WHAT DO YOU THINK THIS MEANS? HAVE YOU EVER EXPERIENCED THIS AS A VISITOR OR WHEN YOU WERE ILL? HOW WOULD YOU DESCRIBE THE FEELING?

▼ The concern and company of young visitors can bring great pleasure to an elderly person who is confined to bed.

▲ Jewish tradition teaches that visiting the sick is a mitzvah, a holy act.

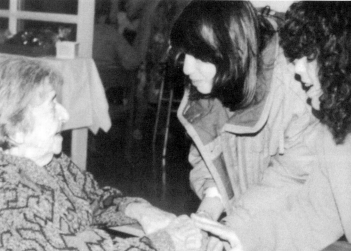

Understanding Our Fears

Most of us feel comfortable visiting someone whose injury or illness will heal within a few weeks or months—a broken wrist or leg, tonsillitis, the flu. But we may feel shy or even repulsed when the injury or illness is more serious—head wounds from a car accident, burns from a fire, long-term depression. And, out of ignorance or fear, we may even avoid someone with a disfiguring or life-threatening disease, such as stroke, cancer, or AIDS. Such resistance to visiting people suffering from more serious illnesses is quite common.

◆ *We may be afraid of illness and death.* Watching someone wrestle with a serious illness can be terrifying. It may conjure up the thought, "That will be me someday." Visiting someone who is seriously ill or dying forces us to recognize that each of us will die some day, a fact that most of us would rather ignore.

You are young, and you will most likely have a long and healthy life. But if you are uncomfortable visiting someone who is gravely ill, you can either make the visit accompanied by a friend or relative, or make a caring phone call instead.

Self-Portrait

★ WHEN I'M NOT FEELING WELL, WHAT I MOST WANT IS FOR SOMEONE TO _____

_____

★ MY WORST INJURY OR ILLNESS WAS

_____

WHAT WAS MOST UPSETTING WAS _____

_____

BECAUSE _____

_____

WHAT I APPRECIATED MOST WAS _____

_____

BECAUSE _____

_____

★ WHEN SOMEONE I CARE ABOUT IS SICK, IF I CAN'T VISIT THE PERSON, WHAT I LIKE TO DO IS _____

★ I THINK THE MOST IMPORTANT THING THAT A CARING FRIEND CAN DO FOR SOMEONE WHO IS ILL IS TO _____

_____

BECAUSE _____

_____

Lending A Hand

The Talmud recounts an occasion when Rabbi Ḥanina visited Rabbi Yoḥanan, a friend and former student, who was ill. After conversing for a while, Rabbi Ḥanina said, "Give me your hand." Rabbi Yoḥanan gave him his hand, and Rabbi Ḥanina raised him from the bed. What makes this story remarkable is that Rabbi Yoḥanan was himself well-known as a holy man who could heal others. If he could heal the sick, then why couldn't he heal himself? The Talmud responds that "the prisoner cannot free himself."

▼ Sometimes what we need to give people who are ill or who have special needs is the simple respect of getting up from our seat on a crowded bus or not parking in a spot reserved for them.

◆ *We fear a loss of control.* When visiting the sick, we are forced to acknowledge that many aspects of life are beyond human control—that health and fitness, indeed, life itself, are gifts. We may at best be able to affect them positively by taking good care of ourselves.

◆ *We are uncomfortable discussing personal concerns.* We rarely reveal our personal hopes and fears to other people. Instead, we seek ways to be distracted together. We watch movies and television shows, listen to music, and play computer games and team sports in the company of others but with little or no conversation. At a sickbed there is no alternative but to speak with one another. At a hospital, the distraction of activities cannot provide an escape from the discomfort we feel.

Check Your Priorities

Often, we may fail to observe the mitzvah of *bikkur ḥolim* simply because we are lazy or distracted. We may decide to finish a book we're reading instead of shlepping to a hospital. Or, overwhelmed by our workload, we may forget that a dear friend, grandparent, or teacher needs our concern and attention. While none of us can be perfect, each of us can regularly check our priorities to ensure that the choices we are making reflect the people we want to be.

We must make the effort to perform the mitzvah of *bikkur ḥolim.* Because only the attention of a friend, relative, or member of the community can reassure the sick that they are still in our thoughts and that we stand ready to help them, we must work to overcome our discomfort, anxieties, and laziness.

Bikkur ḥolim is a mitzvah that can be performed for everyone who ails—the young and the old, the poor and the rich, the simple and the learned, the Jew and the non-Jew. The steps that follow can help you provide this important care.

Ready! Set! GO!

Make a call or send an e-mail. One basic act of *bikkur ḥolim* is paying attention when a friend or classmate is ill and out of school. A call or e-mail from you could be just the right medicine at such a time. Find out how your friend is doing, offer to e-mail or drop off homework assignments, or just chat about what's been happening. We all appreciate knowing that we're on someone's mind. We all feel flattered when others take the time to keep in touch.

Send a card or a note. It may be impossible to phone or visit someone. But don't allow silence to isolate the sick—send a note. You don't need to provide false cheer; just sending a note as brief as "I'm thinking of you" or "We want you to know that we love you" can be a great morale booster to someone who is ill.

◀ **Pampering a friend who is ill by doing her hair can be lots of fun and a mitzvah!**

Visit. There is no substitute for the physical presence of caring people; it can banish the blues and encourage hopefulness. A close friend or family member of someone who is seriously ill should visit immediately. Others should wait several days (the Talmud suggests waiting three days) before visiting.

▲ **Volunteers bring medicine, food, and moral support to people whose homes were destroyed in a flood.**

Phone ahead (or call a family member) to check that it is a convenient time to visit. This simple gesture creates the anticipation of a visit, giving the sick person that much more pleasure.

Don't plan on staying long. Sick people often tire easily. It is better to visit briefly but repeatedly than to visit once for a long time. When the patient tires, leave courteously with a promise to return another time.

◆ *Prayer can be informal.* A simple wish of *refu'ah sh'leimah* ("a complete healing") may bring a level of comfort that ordinary conversation cannot. Jewish tradition offers a brief prayer linking the experience of the individual to the broader community: "May God show compassion to you, together with all the other sick of the people of Israel and of the inhabitants of the world."

◆ *If possible, visit before Shabbat or a holiday and bring an item that will help the patient celebrate.* On a Friday, consider bringing two ḥallah rolls. Before Purim, bring some hamantashen; for Rosh Hashanah, provide honey and apples; and on Passover offer matzah and a haggadah. Linking your visits to the Jewish holidays can help the person feel reconnected to life beyond the sickroom.

▲ Singer and songwriter Debbie Friedman has composed a song of healing, "Mi Shebeirach," based on the traditional blessing for those who are ill. It is sung in many synagogues, summer camps, retreats, homes, and other places where Jews gather to pray.

4 **Bring a gift that can raise the patient's spirits.** When possible, bring something to help distract the person from his or her illness or injury. For example, you might bring a CD of the person's favorite music, a humorous book or tape, or a game that can be played by one or two people. Use your good judgment in choosing something appropriate. For example, if the person has an eye injury, a book may not be the most useful gift. Instead, buy an audio book or create one with other family members or with friends.

5 **Offer to observe a Jewish ritual or to recite a prayer with the patient.** The rabbis of the Talmud often made a point of praying in the presence of the sick, some even claiming that a visit that did not include a prayer did not constitute *bikkur ḥolim.*

▲ If you are working on a school or synagogue play or a talent show, consider performing or rehearsing it at a local nursing home or hospital on a holiday, such as Ḥanukkah or Purim. How else can you make the mitzvah of bikkur ḥolim part of your holiday celebrations?

▲ Both adults and teens at B'nai Israel, a synagogue in Millburn, New Jersey, love to clown around, especially for a good cause! After studying Jewish texts on working with the sick, they learn how to be "mitzvah clowns"—how to sport squeaky noses, wield squirting cameras, and generally be silly for the pleasure and healing of patients in hospitals and nursing homes.

Consider organizing a group performance at a nursing home or hospital, perhaps by your synagogue choir, school orchestra, or dance class. Or, your youth group could conduct a *havdalah* service at a health facility for the elderly.

8 Form a junior bikkur ḥolim committee or join your synagogue's adult committee. Many synagogues have a committee that is informed when someone from the congregation is ill. Members of such committees regularly phone and visit those who are ailing, as well as their families. This can reassure such people that they are not alone and that the Jewish community pays attention and cares about them. The members of a *bikkur ḥolim* committee often find creative ways in which to express their caring. For example, they may cook food for the family, take the patient's children to a movie or sports event, or cover while the caregiver has a few hours to himself or herself.

6 Contribute tzedakah in honor of the sick person. Contributing tzedakah in honor of someone who is ill is a Jewish way of demonstrating concern and respect for that person.

7 Visit nursing home residents, longtime hospital patients, and elderly shut-ins. Many people with chronic illness suffer for such a long time, we may forget that they continue to need our concern and attention. The mitzvah of *bikkur ḥolim* applies to these people too.

It's a Dilemma!

WHEN WE VISIT OR PHONE SOMEONE WHO IS ILL, WE TRY TO BE OUR MOST PLEASANT AND FRIENDLY SELVES. BUT SOME PEOPLE HAVE DIFFICULT PERSONALITIES OR BECOME SHORT-TEMPERED WHEN THEY ARE IN PAIN.

IMAGE THAT YOU ARE VISITING A RELATIVE WHO IS ILL AND THAT HE OR SHE BECOMES SHORT-TEMPERED OR IS RUDE. HOW MIGHT YOU HANDLE THE SITUATION?

_____

_____

_____

_____

WOULD YOU BE WILLING TO VISIT THE PERSON AGAIN? WHY OR WHY NOT?

_____

_____

_____

WHAT MIGHT YOU DO TO AVOID SUCH PROBLEMS IN THE FUTURE?

_____

_____

_____

_____

_____

think about it!

SOMETIMES WHAT AT FIRST SEEMS INAPPROPRIATE MAY TURN OUT TO BE THE "BEST MEDICINE." RABBI AARON LEVINE TELLS THE STORY OF A WOMAN WHO BROUGHT A RAINCOAT AS A GIFT TO AN AILING FRIEND IN THE HOSPITAL. SHE SAID TO THE PATIENT, "THE WEATHER IS BAD. SOON YOU'LL NEED THE RAINCOAT."

WHAT DO YOU THINK THE VISITOR HOPED TO ACCOMPLISH WITH HER GIFT? DO YOU THINK IT WAS A GOOD IDEA? WHY OR WHY NOT?

Rabbi Akiva's Lesson

The Talmud tells a story about Rabbi Akiva and a student who was ill. When Akiva discovered that no one was attending to the student's needs, he went to the student's home and ordered his other students to clean the house.

Because of their care, the student recovered more quickly. In gratitude, the student said to Rabbi Akiva, "My master, you have revived me." Immediately Rabbi Akiva taught that "a person who does not visit the sick is comparable to one who sheds the blood of another."

Do you agree or disagree? Why?

_____

_____

_____

_____

Teens
Make a Difference
Alan and Sharon Kohn

Alan and Sharon Kohn live in Omaha, Nebraska. Alan, a high-school senior, is a member of his school's student council, and Sharon, a sophomore, is on the field hockey team. Both are A students, and both volunteer as teacher assistants in their synagogue's Sunday school.

This brother and sister team chose to work with six-year-old cardiac patients from a nearby children's hospital to create a mural for the hospital and, in the process, give the kids a good time.

Their goal wasn't easy to achieve. It required patience when the children didn't understand the directions or—even more frustrating—when they didn't want to follow the directions. It also demanded a positive attitude and tremendous organization to keep everyone on task. But the teens stuck to it. They worked with the hospital's professional staff, and when they made mistakes they were not disheartened by them. Instead, the teens made plans for what they would do better next time.

Alan and Sharon were impressed by the spirit of the young patients. They learned a great deal about what the hospital does for children and were thrilled with the finished mural. Their advice to other teens: "Don't be afraid to get out there and try things you've never done before; mistakes are inevitable for even the most experienced leader." ☼

▶ The ideal of loving your neighbors comes from the ideal of love of family. Working with a brother or sister on a bikkur holim project can help you move closer to both ideals.

To deepen my commitment to the mitzvah of *bikkur ḥolim*, I chose to _____

_____

because _____

_____

This is what I did (provide a detailed description): _____

_____

_____

I would/wouldn't choose to do this again because _____

_____

What I learned about myself by performing the mitzvah of *bikkur ḥolim* is _____

_____

_____

I think that performing this mitzvah can/cannot help me become the adult I want to

become because _____

_____

My other thoughts on observing this mitzvah: _____

_____

_____

_____

_____

_____

_____

⑪ Kibbud Av Va'em

the most difficult mitzvah?

When a person honors parents, God says, "I consider it as though I lived with them and they honored Me."

—Talmud, Kiddushin 30b

Relating to our parents is a tricky business. It always has been. It always will be.

In our infancy, our parents have total control over us. When they feed us, we eat. When they change our diapers, we are clean. When they clothe us, we are warm and protected. As toddlers and young children, our parents' schedules, preferences, and priorities continue to shape our lives. But as we grow into adolescence the balance starts to shift. We begin to assert authority over when we will come home, with whom we will form friendships, and to which activities we will devote our greatest attention.

They Gave Us Life and Continue to Sustain Us

The natural cycle of growth and maturity, and the shifting balance of authority notwithstanding, Jewish tradition places great emphasis on *kibbud* (literally, "honor"—the way we act) and *yirah* (literally, "reverence"—our intentions) toward parents. It teaches that our parents merit our honor and respect, for they are the people who gave us life itself and then continued to devote years of care and love to us.

Through the countless acts of devotion that are part of child rearing, loving parents demonstrate that the world is a reliable and basically good place. Each time mothers comfort screaming babies, each time fathers feed hungry infants, children are reassured that they are not alone, that their needs are important and will be met, and that compassion and love are real and powerful. In nurturing their children, parents establish the emotional base for future sacred relationships, such as those with a life partner, with the community, and with God.

These people—our parents—also link us to our sacred past, our culture, and our Covenant with God. The childhood memories of lighting Ḥanukkah candles, the smell of fresh-baked ḥallah, the joy and love of a Passover seder—all of these connections to Judaism are transmitted through our parents.

▲ The endless hours of love, teaching, and sharing that good parenting involves is a gift so complete that Judaism asks us to spend the rest of our lives honoring our parents with gratitude and appreciation.

Honor vs. Love

Although the Torah records the mitzvah of *honoring* parents, nowhere in Jewish tradition are children commanded to *love* them. Focusing on deeds of honor, Jewish tradition says nothing about whether or not we owe love to those who gave us life. Why is this so?

Some would claim that emotions are spontaneous and uncontrollable. Yet we cultivate and direct our emotions all the time—toward relatives, friends, school, and country, for example. Indeed, the Torah commands love of God, of other Jews, and of non-Jews. So why doesn't the Torah or Talmud mandate love of parents?

▲ As well as being a part of our tradition, Jewish holy days are in many ways a gift from our parents. By teaching us how to celebrate festivals such as Sukkot and Passover, our parents help us add joy, gratitude, and meaning to the cycle of each year.

RABBI SHIMON BAR YOHAI SAID, "THE MOST DIFFICULT OF ALL MITZVOT IS 'HONOR YOUR PARENTS.'"
—*Tanhumah, Ekev 2*

DO YOU AGREE OR DISAGREE? WHY?

_____

_____

_____

_____

Perhaps it is because there is no relationship as multilayered and deep as the one between parent and child. Even our relationship with a spouse doesn't acquire the complex psychological significance that a relationship with a parent has. Experiences of total dependency, of complete rebellion, and of becoming increasingly similar to one's parents are all commonplace between the generations. Spouses can divorce and friends can separate, but parents are forever.

▲ Sometimes, even when we know our parents are trying to be supportive—for example, by helping us prepare for a test—we may feel unfairly pressured or judged by them. If this should happen, how can you respectfully communicate your feelings?

Given the complexity that characterizes the parent-child relationship, it would be impossible to reduce the bundle of feelings it includes to any single emotion, such as love, rage, or acceptance, or to expect that the feelings will always be controlled. But *behavior* can be controlled, reined in, and directed, and respect and honor are legitimate demands even as emotions fluctuate and perhaps contradict one another. For that reason, Jewish tradition focuses on the practical question of how children *treat* parents rather than attempting to regulate how children *feel* about their parents, an impossible task from the start.

▲ Given how complex parent-child relationships are, how can you develop a clear picture of your family?

Self-Portrait

Rabbi Abraham Joshua Heschel said, "In so many cases, it is the parents who make it impossible for the young to obey the Fifth Commandment. My message to parents is: Every day ask yourselves the question: 'What is there about me that deserves the reverence of my child?'"

Jewish tradition does not support abusive behavior regardless of whether it is carried out by a parent or by a child. Instead, it teaches that every human being has the right to dignity and respect. The mitzvah of *yirah* is appropriately extended to a parent who routinely violates this right to the degree that revering the parent encourages the child not to respond to the abuse with abuse. *Yirah* also implies that children should try to remain open to true regret and repentance on the part of formerly abusive parents.

I AM SIMILAR TO MY PARENTS IN THE FOLLOWING WAYS:

_____

_____

I AM DIFFERENT FROM MY PARENTS IN THE FOLLOWING WAYS: _____

_____

I AM SIMILAR TO MY FRIENDS IN THE FOLLOWING WAYS:

_____

_____

I AM DIFFERENT FROM MY FRIENDS IN THE FOLLOWING WAYS: _____

_____

I AM MORE INDEPENDENT NOW THAN TWO YEARS AGO IN THE FOLLOWING WAYS: _____

_____

I AM STILL DEPENDENT ON MY PARENTS IN THE FOLLOWING WAYS: _____

_____

IN TWO YEARS, I HOPE TO BE INDEPENDENT IN THE FOLLOWING WAYS: _____

_____

⭐ My Attitudes

THE WORDS THAT BEST DESCRIBE MY ATTITUDES TOWARD MY MOTHER ARE:

(CHECK AS MANY RESPONSES AS ARE APPROPRIATE)

_____ LOVING	_____ SELFISH	_____ RESPECTFUL	_____ ARROGANT
_____ HURTFUL	_____ KIND	_____ HUTZPADIK	_____ THOUGHTFUL
_____ COOPERATIVE	_____ CARING	_____ RESENTFUL	_____ POLITE
_____ UNDERSTANDING	_____ UNGRATEFUL	_____ UNPREDICTABLE	_____ OPEN

OTHER: _____

⭐ My Actions

I SPEAK TO MY MOTHER IN THE TONE OF VOICE THAT I WANT TO BE SPOKEN TO:

_____ ALWAYS _____ USUALLY _____ SOMETIMES _____ INFREQUENTLY _____ NEVER

I RESPOND AS QUICKLY TO MY MOTHER'S REQUESTS AS I WANT HER TO RESPOND TO MINE:

_____ ALWAYS _____ USUALLY _____ SOMETIMES _____ INFREQUENTLY _____ NEVER

I EXTEND MORE RESPECT TO MY MOTHER THAN I DEMAND FROM HER:

_____ ALWAYS _____ USUALLY _____ SOMETIMES _____ INFREQUENTLY _____ NEVER

ONE ATTITUDE I CAN CHANGE TO IMPROVE MY RELATIONSHIP WITH MY MOTHER IS

_____

ONE BEHAVIOR I CAN CHANGE TO IMPROVE MY RELATIONSHIP WITH MY MOTHER IS

_____

ONE BEHAVIOR I WISH MY MOTHER WOULD CHANGE IS

_____

IT WOULD IMPROVE OUR RELATIONSHIP BECAUSE

_____

My Attitudes

THE WORDS THAT BEST DESCRIBE MY ATTITUDES TOWARD MY FATHER ARE:

(CHECK AS MANY RESPONSES AS ARE APPROPRIATE)

_____ LOVING	_____ SELFISH	_____ RESPECTFUL	_____ ARROGANT
_____ HURTFUL	_____ KIND	_____ HUTZPADIK	_____ THOUGHTFUL
_____ COOPERATIVE	_____ CARING	_____ RESENTFUL	_____ POLITE
_____ UNDERSTANDING	_____ UNGRATEFUL	_____ UNPREDICTABLE	_____ OPEN

OTHER:_____

My Actions

I SPEAK TO MY FATHER IN THE TONE OF VOICE THAT I WANT TO BE SPOKEN TO:

_____ ALWAYS   _____ USUALLY   _____ SOMETIMES   _____ INFREQUENTLY   _____ NEVER

I RESPOND AS QUICKLY TO MY FATHER'S REQUESTS AS I WANT HIM TO RESPOND TO MINE:

_____ ALWAYS   _____ USUALLY   _____ SOMETIMES   _____ INFREQUENTLY   _____ NEVER

I EXTEND MORE RESPECT TO MY FATHER THAN I DEMAND FROM HIM:

_____ ALWAYS   _____ USUALLY   _____ SOMETIMES   _____ INFREQUENTLY   _____ NEVER

ONE ATTITUDE I CAN CHANGE TO IMPROVE MY RELATIONSHIP WITH MY FATHER IS

_____

ONE BEHAVIOR I CAN CHANGE TO IMPROVE MY RELATIONSHIP WITH MY FATHER IS

_____

ONE BEHAVIOR I WISH MY FATHER WOULD CHANGE IS

_____

IT WOULD IMPROVE OUR RELATIONSHIP BECAUSE

_____

Families come in all shapes and sizes, and there is no one, perfect way to be. However, showing respect for your parents can help inspire the peace and mutual trust that makes family life a blessing.

Ready! Set! GO!

Here are some ways you can fulfill the mitzvah of *kibbud av va'em.*

1 Make your parents a priority.

As a teen, your life may well be filled with a host of commitments—school, sports teams, Junior Congregation, volunteer work, youth group, parties, baby-sitting, and music lessons. But before completely filling up your schedule, be sure to leave time to lend a hand at home, time to notice how your parents are doing, and to acknowledge that their needs matter too.

◆ *Pay attention!* Is your dad exhausted or worried about your grandmother's health? Are pressures at your mom's job or her allergies making it stressful to meet car pool or other obligations? Is your parents' anniversary coming up or a birthday being celebrated? Have you slipped into the fantasy that only you have a life, that only you have feelings?

◆ *Take an action!* When your parents are feeling tired, stressed, or blue, give them a hug and tell them how much you love them. (In fact, give them that hug for no particular reason!) Be thoughtful, and ask not "if" but "how" you can be of help. Mark their birthdays and anniversary on your calendar so that you remember to prepare a card and gift in advance, not at the last moment when you may forget or will have limited choices.

▲ Think about how much you appreciate a home-baked birthday cake or a special meal cooked in your honor. Double that feeling, and you will have some idea of how thrilled parents feel when their children do the same thing for them.

Making your parents a priority does not mean giving up the other important relationships and commitments you have. It means showing respect for your parents' needs, values, and concerns, as well as for your own. And it means showing gratitude for the many ways in which your parents do their best to give you both what you need and what you want.

Speak respectfully to your parents, even when disagreeing with them. Children may, and should, assert their self-worth and stand up for the right to hold their own opinions and still receive decent treatment. Still, *yirah* implies that disagreements with parents should not involve public forums or unnecessary hostility. In other words, name-calling, vulgar language, threats, and violence are never acceptable. Children owe parents a respectful, restrained, and dignified presentation of their feelings and opinions.

It's difficult to do, but you can disagree with your parents and still exhibit *yirah* and *kibbud*. When you disagree, use a calm tone of voice and civil language. Try to imagine your parents' perspective. What reasonable concern might motivate them to take the position they do? How can you ease their concern? Choose a time and place that permit leisurely and private discussion. In a quiet moment, you might explain what your parents can do to help make disagreements less anxiety producing and tense. These guidelines can also serve you well in other relationships.

Retain a distinction between the generations. We live in an age of militant equality. Everyone is the equal of everyone else, regardless of talent, training, and commitment. We attack hierarchy in any form. One of the few remaining areas of authority is that of parents with regard to children: Parents and children may be equal as valued human beings, but they are still not equals in authority.

Although most children will become independent individuals with the ability to live their own lives, they will never be their parents' peers.

4 **Ask yourself, "Do I expect my parents to be perfect?"** As we grow up, we insist on the right to go our own way, and we expect to be forgiven for our mistakes, asserting that we're only human. Yet we often hold our parents to an impossibly high standard, expecting them to be perfect.

▲ Why do you think "Honor your father and mother" is one of the Ten Commandments? (Can you identify which commandment it is?) If you could add an eleventh commandment about how parents should treat their children, what would the commandment be?

▲ Would you want your parents to treat you as an equal? What do you think the pluses or minuses of their doing so would be?

Most parents cannot live up to all of their *own* expectations, let alone to the expectations their children have of them. Difficult though it may be, recognizing that your parents are human and therefore imperfect, that they are often not in control of what happens, and that they work hard to do their best can help you treat them with honor and respect, even when you don't share their priorities or like the way they behave.

5 **Look for ways to adapt to the house rules.** Just as you look forward to creating your own home and establishing the standards and values it will reflect, so must you now be respectful of your parents' choices. You may not like the curfew your parents have set, or agree with decisions to save on energy bills or limit telephone and TV time; you may not think that it's important to empty the trash as often as your parents demand. But for now, you live in the home your parents created based on *their* hopes, dreams, and values (not to mention maintained through their hard work and money); try to behave accordingly.

▲ Thoughtful actions, such as calling home when you are delayed, can not only help you avoid arguments with your parents but also can help your parents develop confidence in your maturity and sense of responsibility.

It's a Dilemma!

YOU AND YOUR FAMILY ARE VISITING FRIENDS, AND ONE OF YOUR PARENTS MAKES A COMMENT THAT EMBARRASSES AND UPSETS YOU BECAUSE IT SOUNDS BIGOTED TO YOU. ON THE ONE HAND, YOU WANT TO STAND UP FOR YOUR IDEALS. ON THE OTHER HAND, YOU WANT TO HONOR YOUR PARENT, NOT EMBARRASS HIM OR HER. WHAT WOULD YOU LIKE TO SAY OR DO? WHY?

_____

_____

_____

WHAT MIGHT BE ANOTHER STRATEGY?

_____

_____

_____

IN WHAT WAYS SHOULD THE HONOR AND RESPECT DUE PARENTS BE EXTENDED TO GRANDPARENTS? TO TEACHERS? TO OTHER ADULTS?

To deepen my commitment to the mitzvah of *kibbud av va'em*, I chose to _____

_____

because_____

_____

This is what I did (provide a detailed description) _____

_____

_____

_____

I would/wouldn't choose to do this again because _____

_____

I think the most important way to honor a parent is _____

because _____

_____

What I learned about myself by performing this mitzvah is _____

_____

For me, the most difficult part of observing *kibbud av va'em* is _____

_____ because _____

_____

My other thoughts on observing this mitzvah: _____

_____

_____

_____

_____

12 Sh'mirat Halashon
weigh your words

May God keep my tongue from evil, my lips from lies.

—Talmud, Berachot 17a

"Join us." "We miss you." "You're wonderful." "We'll help." "I love you."

Words are powerful. They can mend an aching heart, soothe a troubled soul, and bring joy and hope to those who grieve. But words don't always heal and comfort; they can also brutalize and scar. Like arrows shot from a hunter's bow, words can pierce even the most calloused skin. Once they have been set in motion, words are hard—if not impossible—to retrieve.

Knowing the staying power of words, why do we sometimes give in to impulse, mocking or humiliating others in the heat of the moment? Why are we willing to gossip, knowing how deeply it can wound? Why can we be quick to lie when it serves us, yet express outrage when others do the same?

A Matter of Courage

It often takes courage to resist the impulse to pass on false information ("Just say I'm not at home"), speak harsh words, or gossip. At certain moments, we may feel that it is the only way to protect ourselves from another's unkind words or unfair accusations. Or, we may worry that friends will think us uncool if we don't join in a put-down, a stretching of the truth, or gossip; if we don't laugh at jokes or incidents that make others look foolish. Our fear of becoming the butt of a joke, our desire for acceptance, and the sheer weight of peer pressure (after all, everybody does it) may lead us to rationalize our lack of courage rather than to stand up for what we know is right. Unfortunately, the more we choose "the path of least resistance," the less likely we are to become the adults of our dreams—the self-confident adults who operate out of inner strength, personal conviction, and integrity.

We all pay a price for the web of gossip, rumors, and deception that we weave: we lose our trust in those around us; we begin to look at people with a skepticism that borders on hostility. In addition, we expect less from others and from ourselves, and we tend to interpret everyone's actions in the worst possible light.

"NOT EVERYTHING THAT IS THOUGHT SHOULD BE EXPRESSED, NOT EVERYTHING THAT IS EXPRESSED VERBALLY SHOULD BE WRITTEN, AND NOT EVERYTHING THAT IS WRITTEN SHOULD BE PUBLISHED."
—*Rabbi Israel Salanter*

THINK OF A TIME WHEN YOU STOPPED YOURSELF FROM SAYING SOMETHING HURTFUL TO OR ABOUT SOMEONE. WHAT WAS GOING ON? HOW DID YOU FEEL AFTERWARD?

_____

_____

_____

_____

_____

"DEATH AND LIFE ARE IN THE POWER OF THE TONGUE."
—*Proverbs 18:21*

WHAT MIGHT A LITERAL UNDERSTANDING OF THIS PROVERB BE? HOW ELSE COULD IT BE INTERPRETED?

◄ Using the gift of speech to stand up for what we know is right takes integrity and strength of character. The megillah we read on Purim tells of Queen Esther, who courageously spoke up before King Ahasuerus, revealing Haman's plan to kill the Jews.

An Evil Tongue

L'shon hara (literally, "the evil tongue") is a derogatory, untrue, or damaging statement that is said for a mean or hurtful purpose. Even *honest* information becomes *l'shon hara* if the primary intention of the teller is negative. Therefore, a joke about a minority group, a story about a foolish or stupid or unkind deed, or a deception are all examples of *l'shon hara.*

There is no easy way to put an end to all *l'shon hara*, but we certainly can limit its spread. When we observe the mitzvah of *sh'mirat halashon*, we strengthen our integrity and character, and we help create a more compassionate community in which people support and trust one another.

▲ While the human failings of others may seem humorous, at times, few of us enjoy having people laugh at our own foibles. Empathy and compassion dictate that we not delight in the embarrassment of others.

Ancient Teachings for Modern Life

● ● ● ● ● ● ● ● ● ● ● ● ● ● ● ● ● ● ● ●

The Torah instructs us to refrain from *l'shon hara.*

לֹא תִשָּׂא שֵׁמַע שָׁוְא...

Do not carry false rumors... (Exodus 23:1)

לֹא תְקַלֵּל חֵרֵשׁ...

Do not insult the deaf... (Leviticus 19:14)

לֹא תֵלֵךְ רָכִיל בְּעַמֶּיךָ...

Do not go about as a talebearer among your people... (Leviticus 19:16)

Why do you think our tradition asks us to study the teachings of the Torah again and again, throughout our lives?

_____

_____

● ●

It's a Mitzvah to Spare Someone's Feelings

Remember: Even a true statement is considered *l'shon hara* if someone is hurt when it is made. For example, in the Bible when our matriarch Sarah hears that she will become pregnant, she laughs and says that both she and Abraham are too old to produce children. God overhears and asks Abraham why Sarah laughed and said that *she* was too old to bear a child, for "is anything too wondrous for Adonai?" (*Genesis 18:13–14*). By altering Sarah's statement, God fulfilled the mitzvah of maintaining *sh'lom bayit* (peace in the family).

Describe a circumstance in which it would be *l'shon hara* to tell the truth.

_____

_____

_____

_____

▼ There is a delicate balance between a concern for others and an indulgence in gossip.

A well-known folk story emphasizes that it is as impossible to take back gossip and other unkind words as it is to collect feathers that have been scattered to the wind.

Indeed, prevention is better than any cure.

Ready! Set! GO!

1 Pray. Each morning, recite this prayer by the 19th-century Polish rabbi Israel Kagan: "Gracious and merciful God, help me restrain myself from speaking or listening to derogatory, damaging, or hostile speech. I will try not to engage in *l'shon hara,* either about individuals or about an entire group of people. I will strive not to say anything that contains falsehood, insincere flattery, scoffing, or elements of needless dispute, anger, arrogance, oppression, or embarrassment to others. Grant me the strength to say nothing unnecessary, so that all my actions and speech cultivate a love for Your creatures and for You."

Pay attention!

Become aware of when you are listening to *l'shon hara* as well as of when you are speaking it. Before making a statement about someone, ask yourself these three questions:

◆ Is it true?
◆ Is it well-intentioned?
◆ Is it unlikely to harm anyone?

If a statement doesn't receive a "yes" to all three questions—put a lid on it! It may be helpful to make a pact with a friend to refrain from speaking *l'shon hara.*

▲ From certain angles, the Tour de Montréal in Canada appears to be toppling over (see photo above). But, that is an illusion (see photo at left). It has simply been designed in a dramatic way. Similarly, when you hear or see something unflattering about another person, consider the possibility that things are not what they seem to be.

▼ Stop and think before you speak!

STOP

▲ While venting your first rush of emotions to a third party can be helpful, expressing your anger, disappointment, or pain directly to the one who provoked it ultimately may be the only way to fully restore trust and honesty, the only way to allow for apologies and improvement. Speaking to each other is always better than speaking about each other.

▲ Jews have often been targets of prejudice and demeaned by anti-Semitic names, such as kike and yid. This experience not only should inspire us to help others who are mistreated but also to reject humor that degrades them.

Cultivate a healthy skepticism about unkind reports of others.

Knowing that each of us sometimes makes statements that are untrue or exaggerated, or that indirectly express our anger, bitterness, or jealousy, consider how free of hostility, insecurity, or embitterment the report is when you hear a person speaking ill of someone.

Keep quiet.

Select the two or three most aggravating people in your life and refrain from speaking about them, especially in public, for at least a week. Generally, discussions about people we don't like are motivated by a desire to demean them or to feel superior to them. But the pleasure we gain from putting them down is always short-lived, while the harm we do and the guilt we experience is likely to last for a long time.

Don't laugh at, or repeat, jokes that degrade others.

Like all *l'shon hara*, jokes about people with special needs, ethnic or religious groups, gender, and sexual preferences demean not only the targets of the jokes, but also the listeners and teller.

Increase your sensitivity to how hurtful l'shon hara can be.

Instead of making a comment about a neighbor, try making the same comment in your head about yourself or a close friend. Does the statement still feel neutral or well-intentioned? If so, it is probably all right to say it about someone else. A similar standard would be to ask yourself, "Would I make this comment in the presence of the person I am speaking about?" If you wouldn't be comfortable making the remark in front of that person, then perhaps you shouldn't make it at all.

 **Balance a derogatory comment with a supportive one.** Because you are human, at times you may say something critical about someone for unkind or self-serving reasons. If it is impossible to undo the remark, try to immediately balance it by expressing your appreciation of a positive trait in that person. This follow-up comment should, of course, be honest, focusing on an admirable characteristic or talent.

 **Ask your family or a close friend to help you create a safe space in which to vent your feelings.** Explain that you want them to listen, not to judge. Most of us have a need to let off steam from time to time because it can help us regain a balanced perspective and sometimes even enable us to forgive others. By limiting whom we share negative feelings with, we limit the harm done to others and remove *l'shon hara* from the realm of social entertainment.

 **If subtle attempts to steer a group away from l'shon hara fail, speak up.** Consider asking the person or group to change the subject, or change it yourself. Be tactful in how you express your unwillingness to participate in gossip. If you don't like being lectured to, don't lecture others. Also, avoid speaking in a self-righteous tone. A brief statement about your needing their help to avoid *l'shon hara* might be the most effective way of persuading people to change the topic. Use an "I" statement, such as, "I'm making a big effort to avoid being critical of others, and I could really use your support."

It's a Dilemma!

YOU ARE HANGING OUT WITH A FEW KIDS FROM SCHOOL. SOMEONE COMMENTS THAT A FRIEND OF THE GROUP (WHO IS NOT PRESENT) HAS BECOME WITHDRAWN AND SHORT-TEMPERED. OTHERS AGREE, ADDING, "HE'S NO FUN ANY MORE," AND "HE'S BECOMING A ROYAL PAIN."

ONLY YOU KNOW THAT THE BOY IN QUESTION HAS BEEN GOING THROUGH A DIFFICULT TIME IN HIS PERSONAL LIFE. WHAT SHOULD YOU DO? SHOULD YOU KEEP SILENT? CHANGE THE SUBJECT? DEFEND HIM BY SHARING WHAT YOU KNOW ABOUT HIS PERSONAL LIFE? FIND ANOTHER SOLUTION?

_____

_____

EXPLAIN WHY YOU THINK THIS WOULD BE A GOOD SOLUTION.

_____

_____

_____

_____

THE JEWISH POET ADRIENNE RICH SAID, "LYING IS DONE WITH WORDS AND ALSO WITH SILENCE."

DO YOU AGREE OR DISAGREE? WHY?

_____

_____

_____

_____

think about it!

WHEN PEOPLE PUT OTHERS DOWN, WHAT ARE THEY SAYING ABOUT THEMSELVES? WHEN YOU PUT SOMEONE DOWN, WHAT ARE YOU REVEALING ABOUT YOURSELF?

★ I WOULD DESCRIBE MYSELF AS HAVING A _____ SENSE OF HUMOR.

★ I LIKE: (CHECK AS MANY RESPONSES AS ARE APPROPRIATE)

_____ TELLING JOKES

_____ LISTENING TO JOKES

_____ RECEIVING E-MAIL LISTS
OF JOKES

_____ STAND-UP COMICS

_____ COMICS WHO DO
IMPRESSIONS

_____ SICK HUMOR

_____ ETHNIC HUMOR

_____ JEWISH HUMOR

_____ SLAPSTICK HUMOR

_____ OFF-COLOR HUMOR

_____ HUMOR THAT USES
GROSS LANGUAGE

_____ DRAWING HUMOROUS
CARTOONS

_____ MAKING UP MY OWN
JOKES

_____ DOING MY OWN HUMOR-
OUS IMPRESSIONS

OTHER: _____

_____

_____

★ I DON'T UNDERSTAND WHY SOME PEOPLE FIND _____ OFFENSIVE.

I THINK IT/HE/SHE/THEY IS/ARE FUNNY BECAUSE _____

_____

★ I DON'T UNDERSTAND WHY SOME PEOPLE FIND _____ FUNNY.

I THINK IT/HE/SHE/THEY IS/ARE _____

BECAUSE _____

_____

★ I THINK THERE SHOULD/SHOULDN'T BE LIMITS TO MOCKING ONESELF OR A MINORITY GROUP

BECAUSE _____

_____

To deepen my commitment to the mitzvah of *sh'mirat halashon*, I chose to _____

_____

because _____

_____

This is what I did (provide a detailed description): _____

_____

_____

_____

I would/wouldn't choose to do this again because _____

_____

What I learned about myself by performing this mitzvah is _____

_____

_____

For me, the most difficult part of observing this mitzvah is _____

_____

because _____

_____

My other thoughts on observing this mitzvah: _____

_____

_____

_____

_____

_____

(13) Tefillah

an open line

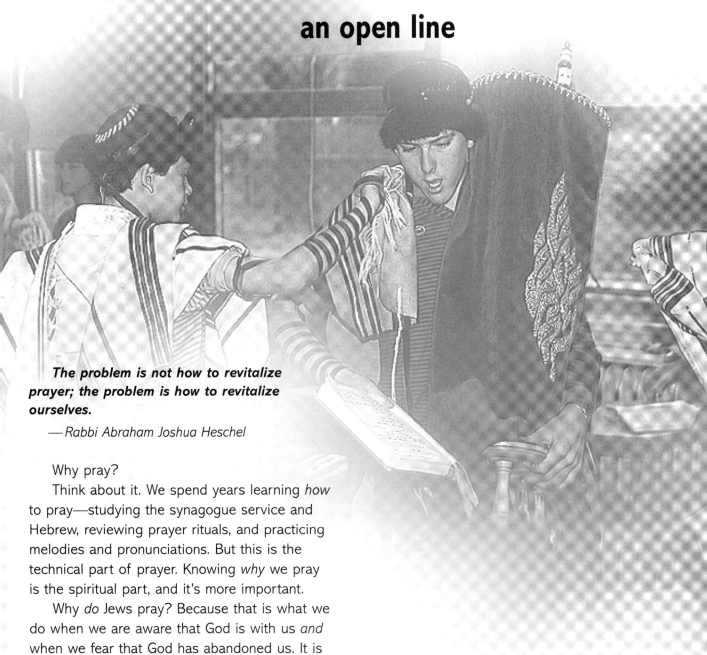

The problem is not how to revitalize prayer; the problem is how to revitalize ourselves.

—Rabbi Abraham Joshua Heschel

Why pray?

Think about it. We spend years learning *how* to pray—studying the synagogue service and Hebrew, reviewing prayer rituals, and practicing melodies and pronunciations. But this is the technical part of prayer. Knowing *why* we pray is the spiritual part, and it's more important.

Why *do* Jews pray? Because that is what we do when we are aware that God is with us *and* when we fear that God has abandoned us. It is how we express our gratitude and our faith, as well as our disappointments and our doubts. It is how we form a bridge to God and how we ask God to meet us halfway across the bridge.

Sacred Footprints

Like the footprints in the sand that are the telltale signs of a person we do not see, the wonders of nature signal God's awesome presence in the world around us. Judaism teaches us to recognize these signs in the fiery glow of an autumn sunset, the silky skin of a newborn baby, and the small acts of kindness that one person does for another. A central goal of Jewish prayer is to heighten our awareness of holiness in our lives and to help us respond with awe and with gratitude.

Reciting Hamotzi before eating focuses us on the abundance we have been given and reminds us that we are the tenants and caretakers, not the owners, of God's world. On Passover, the blessings over maror and other foods focus us on the gift of freedom we received, reminding us that we were redeemed from the bitterness of slavery so that we could serve God. And the V'shamru prayer focuses us on the holiness of Shabbat, reminding us that we were given a day of rest as an eternal sign of Creation and our partnership with God.

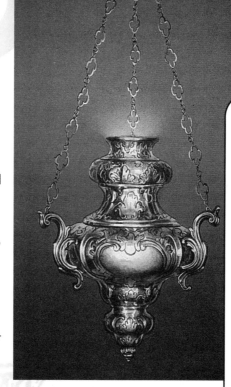

▲ A ner tamid, or eternal light, hangs above the Holy Ark in a synagogue sanctuary. Its constant light symbolizes God's eternal presence.

REMEMBER THE SOURCE OF ALL CREATION

The Talmud teaches us that one who eats without saying a blessing commits an act of theft, stealing what belongs to God.

Letting God In

The pious rabbi Ḥasid Mendel of Kotzk once asked a group of learned guests, "Where does God dwell?" Surprised by his question, they responded, "Is not the whole world filled with God's glory?"

Shaking his head, the rabbi said, "God dwells wherever we let God in."

This story reminds us that we have a partnership with God. On the one hand, we are never far from God's holy presence, for God can be everywhere. On the other hand, God waits for our willingness to "open the door."

In this space, draw a picture or write a poem that illustrates the actions we can take to open the door and let God in.

What We Pray For

Judaism teaches us to pray for what we want to become—not for what we want to be given. Praying for a good grade on a test cannot help. But praying for the willingness to study can. Praying for a sports trophy cannot help. But praying for the patience to practice can. And praying for blue eyes when you have brown eyes, or brown when you have blue, cannot help. But praying for the willingness to appreciate our God-given beauty and talents can.

Are there times when you pray in synagogue but have difficulty connecting to the words you are saying? How could silently praying by thinking about your life—the personal choices you have made, the way you treat the people you love, the way you treat those you would prefer to avoid but can't—help you figure out how well you are living and how you could improve? Might silently reading a poem or meditation from the prayer book help you express gratitude for the good in your life?

think about it!

Tefillah IS THE HEBREW WORD FOR "PRAYER." IT COMES FROM THE SAME ROOT AS THE WORD MEANING "TO JUDGE." JUDAISM TEACHES THAT WHEN WE PRAY, NOT ONLY DO WE STAND BEFORE GOD, BUT WE ALSO JUDGE OURSELVES. PRAYER HELPS US SEE HOW WELL WE ARE LIVING AS CREATURES MADE IN GOD'S IMAGE AND HOW WE CAN IMPROVE. WHEN WE PRAY, WE PRAISE GOD FOR THE GOOD IN OUR LIVES AND ASK FOR THE WILLINGNESS TO BECOME BETTER PEOPLE.

YOU DON'T SAY!

"IF LIFE IS A BOWL OF CHERRIES, WHAT AM I DOING IN THE PITS?"
—*Erma Bombeck*

HAVE YOU EVER FELT THAT WAY? HOW CAN PRAYING OR RECITING A BLESSING REMIND YOU OF THE GOOD IN YOUR LIFE?

_____

_____

_____

_____

▲ On Sukkot we celebrate the abundance and goodness in our lives by reciting prayers of gratitude and by eating in a sukkah decorated with symbols of the harvest.

Prayer Can Help Us Sort Out Our Emotions

Prayer not only helps us express gratitude and work toward improving our lives, it also helps us sort out our emotions when they threaten to overwhelm us. Think about it. Do you ever feel so excited or relieved by good news that you don't know whether to laugh or cry? Are there times when you feel frightened, confused, or lonely? Are you ever angry with someone you love? Do you sometimes struggle with self-doubts or feelings of jealousy?

Everyone experiences such conflicts and turmoil from time to time. Prayer can calm and focus us so that we can develop a clearer, more realistic picture of what is going on. Prayer can turn feelings of excitement into words of thanks and appreciation. It can comfort us when we despair, feel frightened, or are hurt. And prayer can remind us of God's love so that we can overcome our loneliness, anger, self-doubt, or mistrust.

Did YOU Know? Certain prayers can be said only in a *minyan*, a community of at least ten Jews who have reached the age of bat or bar mitzvah. Two such prayers are Kaddish and Kedushah. Their names come from the same root as the Hebrew word *kadosh*, meaning "holy." When we recite these prayers, we are reminded of the importance of coming together to live as a holy people, an *am kadosh*.

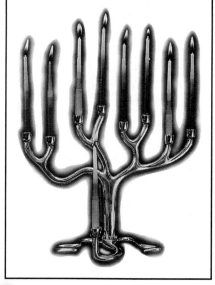

▶ In every country and every age in which Jews have lived, Shabbat prayers have been recited on Friday night. Jews in Argentina, Israel, France, and Greece join us in making seders on the fifteenth of Nisan, the first night of Passover. And, when you chant the blessings over Hanukkah candles, you are doing as Jews did in the time of Columbus and as they still do today, even in places as far away as Brazil and South Africa.

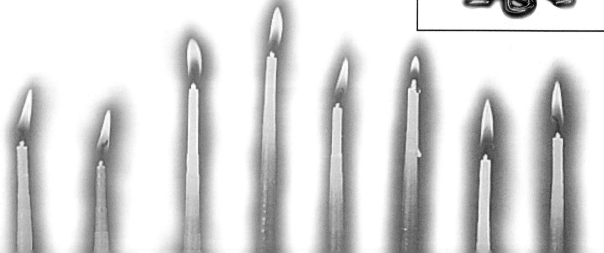

You Are Not Alone

Jewish tradition teaches the value of praying with the community. By praying with others, we are reminded that we are not alone—that we are part of a much larger family. And by participating in synagogue services, we become partners in prayer with the entire community, connected to one another and to God.

▼ **Praying outdoors can help focus us on the wonder of Creation.**

In fact, most Jewish prayers are intended to be recited when we pray as a group. That is why we say, "Blessed are You, *our* God," not "*my* God." That is why we say, "Help *us* lie down in peace," not "Help *me* lie down in peace." Even when we pray by ourselves, we are still not alone. By saying the same words that we recite with our congregation, we are united with Jews throughout the world and throughout time.

Self-Portrait

⭐ I AM MOST LIKELY TO PRAY WHEN I FEEL: (CHECK AS MANY RESPONSES AS ARE APPROPRIATE)

—— HAPPY ⠀⠀⠀ —— NERVOUS ⠀⠀⠀ —— ILL ⠀⠀⠀ OTHER:_____

—— SAD ⠀⠀⠀ —— LONELY ⠀⠀⠀ —— INSECURE ⠀⠀⠀ _____

—— UPSET ⠀⠀⠀ —— CONFUSED ⠀⠀⠀ —— THANKFUL ⠀⠀⠀ _____

⭐ I FEEL BEST PRAYING: (CHECK AS MANY RESPONSES AS ARE APPROPRIATE)

—— IN SYNAGOGUE ⠀⠀⠀⠀⠀ —— WITH MY CONGREGATION

—— BY MYSELF ⠀⠀⠀⠀⠀ —— AT RELIGIOUS SCHOOL

—— IN HEBREW ⠀⠀⠀⠀⠀ —— SILENTLY

—— IN ENGLISH ⠀⠀⠀⠀⠀ —— ALOUD

—— WITH MY FAMILY ⠀⠀⠀⠀⠀ OTHER:_____

—— OUTDOORS ⠀⠀⠀⠀⠀ _____

—— IN MY ROOM ⠀⠀⠀⠀⠀ _____

—— WITH KIDS MY OWN AGE ⠀⠀⠀⠀⠀ _____

⭐ MY FAVORITE PRAYER IN THE SIDDUR IS _____

I LIKE IT BECAUSE _____

_____

Ready! Set! GO!

Here are a few ways to develop your spiritual awareness and strengthen your connection with God through prayer.

1 **Slow down and experience the marvel of the world around you.** Try the following suggestions:

◆ *Consider what the impact would be if just one of nature's wonders disappeared.* For example, what pleasures might you miss if there were no fruit trees? the tangy sweetness of apple pie and prune hamantashen? the beauty and scent of cherry blossoms and orange blooms?

◆ *Make time for experiences you generally miss, or take time to notice the details you ordinarily overlook.* How about waking up in time to watch the sunrise? Try taking an extra moment to close your eyes and enjoy the warmth of the midday sun or the taste of cold water when you are hot and thirsty.

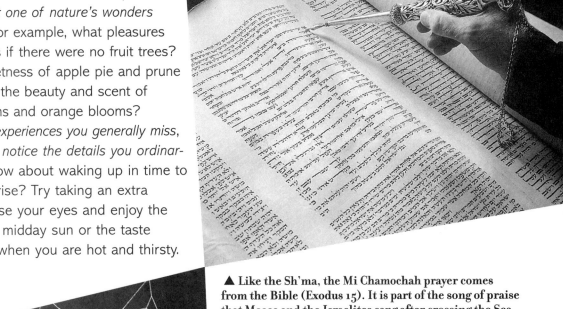

▲ Like the Sh'ma, the Mi Chamochah prayer comes from the Bible (Exodus 15). It is part of the song of praise that Moses and the Israelites sang after crossing the Sea of Reeds. As this photograph shows, the song stands out from the rest of the text.

▲ The delicacy of a spider's web is only one of the many marvels you can observe in the everyday world.

2 **Pray spontaneously.** According to Jewish tradition, "The gates of prayer are always open." The Bible and Talmud record numerous instances when people spoke directly from their hearts to God, revealing their pain, joy, needs, or hopes. Prayer can provide a healthy outlet for our doubts, impatience, and rage, and it can help us acknowledge our love, gratitude, and happiness. It can be said aloud or silently, in the synagogue, at home, in the street, at school, or any place else we find ourselves.

 **Recite the morning and evening Sh'ma.** This biblical verse proclaims, "Hear O Israel: Adonai is our God, Adonai is one" *(Deuteronomy 6:4)*. It reminds us of a central belief of Judaism: we have a relationship with God; God cares about us; and God is unique. Reciting this prayer can be a way to focus yourself in the morning, helping you to move forward centered in your identity, beliefs, and convictions.

 **Recite Hamotzi and Birkat Hamazon regularly.** Expressing appreciation through prayer reminds us how much good there is in our lives. No prayer of gratitude is more basic or typically Jewish than Hamotzi, the blessing before eating.

▲ While it is possible to pray anywhere, attending services at a synagogue has the advantage of strengthening our connection to the Jewish community, as well as strengthening the community's connection to us.

As you become more comfortable reciting Hamotzi and Birkat Hamazon, consider doing so as part of your weekday regime.

Use prayer to make the ordinary extraordinary. Judaism teaches us to become aware of and to celebrate the many wonderful occasions that arise on even the most ordinary of days. The Sheheḥeyanu blessing is an invaluable tool for accomplishing this. At any happy occasion, such as a holiday or the receipt of a great report card, or when enjoying something new, such as an article of clothing or piece of sports equipment, this brief *brachah* thanks God "for granting us life, for sustaining us, and for helping us to reach this day." By reciting the Sheheḥeyanu, you can lend a deeper meaning—the understanding that life is a gift—to anything from the celebration of a birthday to the purchase of a sweater.

▲ It is a practice at many Jewish summer camps to sing z'mirot, or songs, as well as Birkat Hamazon at the end of Shabbat meals. You may want to try this at home to enliven your family's celebration of Shabbat.

After we have eaten and are satisfied, our tradition teaches us to express gratitude again by reciting the Birkat Hamazon. To develop the habit of reciting these blessings, make them part of your Shabbat observance.

6 **Attend Shabbat services regularly for two months.** In time, you will come to know more congregants as well as feel more at ease with the synagogue service. You are likely to gain skill and confidence in reading the prayers and, thus, be able to shift your focus from pronouncing the words to exploring their meaning. If you already regularly attend services, invite a friend who doesn't to join you, or ask a newcomer to sit with you and your family.

▲ Regularly attending Shabbat services can become an important family tradition.

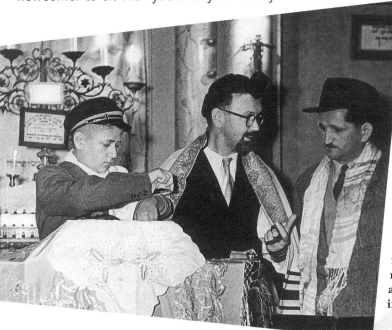

◄ This picture is from Communist Romania in 1960, where it was dangerous for Jews to openly practice Judaism. It shows a bar mitzvah boy, Michael Wasserman, with his rabbi and father. The tallitot (prayer shawls) and tefillin they are wearing were smuggled into Romania by the Israeli embassy.

Follow the Custom

DIFFERENT SYNAGOGUES HAVE DIFFERENT CUSTOMS. FOR EXAMPLE, IN SOME SYNAGOGUES THE ONLY PEOPLE WHO STAND FOR THE MOURNERS' KADDISH ARE THOSE WHO ARE IN MOURNING OR WHO ARE OBSERVING A *yahrtzeit*, THE ANNIVERSARY OF A LOVED ONE'S DEATH. IN OTHER SYNAGOGUES, THE ENTIRE CONGREGATION STANDS FOR THE KADDISH. IN SOME SYNAGOGUES, THE TORAH IS READ ON SHABBAT MORNING. IN OTHERS, IT IS READ ON FRIDAY NIGHT, *erev Shabbat*.

SIMILARLY, DIFFERENT FAMILIES HAVE DIFFERENT CUSTOMS. SOME FAMILIES SING THE HYMN SHALOM ALEICHEM BEFORE THE SHABBAT MEAL; OTHER FAMILIES DO NOT. SOME FAMILIES STAND WHILE KIDDUSH IS RECITED, WHILE OTHER FAMILIES SIT.

WHEN WE ARE VISITING A SYNAGOGUE OR SOMEONE'S HOME, JEWISH TRADITION ASKS US TO OBSERVE THE CUSTOMS OF THAT PLACE, *minhag hamakom*. WE ARE REQUIRED TO BE RESPECTFUL AND COURTEOUS GUESTS.

Prayer as a Reality Check

When something goes wrong in your day—you miss the bus, have a disagreement with a friend, or lose a favorite earring—you may obsess over it for hours. But how often do you focus on the good in your life—the beauty of the world around you, the people who love and care for you, and the talents and personality that make you YOU?

When we don't pay attention to and express gratitude for the good in our lives, it is easy to imagine that we have no luck, that nothing good ever happens to us. Reciting blessings and other prayers can provide a reality check: In the middle of a humdrum or difficult day, prayer can remind us that we have much to be grateful for.

It's a Dilemma!

IN THE MIDDLE OF A BAT MITZVAH SERVICE YOU START THINKING ABOUT A PERSONAL PROBLEM AND BECOME UPSET. YOU DON'T WANT TO BE RUDE AND WALK OUT OF THE SERVICE, BUT YOU FEEL PHONY RECITING THE PRAYERS OF GRATITUDE AND JOY. WHAT DO YOU DO?

_____

_____

WHY DO YOU THINK THIS WOULD BE APPROPRIATE AND HELPFUL?

_____

_____

_____

_____

_____

Prayer Book! Tallit! Ark! Kippah! Action!

A good play requires props, costumes, stage directions, good lighting, the right backdrop, and a little music at the appropriate moment. Each of these elements helps the actors successfully take on the life and personality of the characters they play. So, too, with worship. The prayer book, ceremonies, songs, and ritual objects are, in some sense, tools that help us more completely identify with the role of a holy people.

To deepen my commitment to the mitzvah of *tefillah*, I chose to _____

_____

because _____

_____

This is what I did (provide a detailed description): _____

_____

_____

_____

I would/wouldn't choose to do this again because _____

_____

Three things that I am thankful for and want to acknowledge in prayer are:

_____

_____

_____

What I learned about myself by performing this mitzvah is _____

_____

My other thoughts on observing this mitzvah: _____

_____

_____

_____

_____

_____

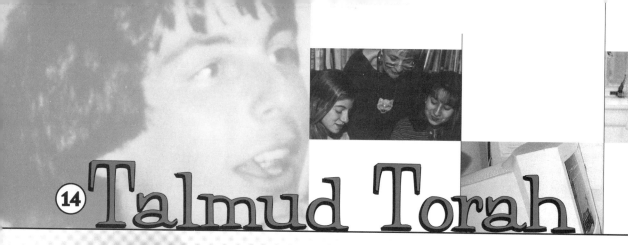

⑭ Talmud Torah

learning matters

> *It is for our own good that we learn Torah and forget it; because if we studied Torah and never forgot it, people would struggle with learning it for two or three years, resume ordinary work, and never pay further attention to it. But because we study Torah and forget it, we don't abandon its study.*
>
> —Kohelet Rabbah 1, 13:1

Imagine dropping out of school after eighth grade. Suppose you never again read a newspaper, novel, or magazine. Suppose you never again went to art exhibits, plays, concerts, or museums. Suppose, for the rest of your life, you had to rely solely on your eighth-grade education to find a job, raise a family, maintain a home, and fulfill the other responsibilities of adulthood. Could you possibly meet the challenge? Would you stand a chance of fulfilling your hopes and dreams?

Now, imagine that, instead, you stopped after high school. Would it make much of a difference?

These thoughts are not so far-fetched. Teens drop out of school all the time and then fail to seek other means of continuing their education. We hear frequent reports about the devastating results to individuals—failure to find steady employment (let alone an interesting job with room for advancement), difficulties in keeping up with technological and social changes, and endless economic hardships, including inadequate housing or even homelessness. In addition, there is a steep cost to society when people fail to realize their potential or to contribute by living fully productive lives.

But what about the effects of dropping out of religious school? of ending Jewish studies as a teen? of not participating in a Jewish youth group or summer camp? How does *that* affect our ability to meet the challenges of adulthood? How does it diminish our capacity to enjoy life and to add joy? How does it impoverish the individual and the community?

▲ Check your local Jewish press for listings of Jewish and Israeli film festivals.

The Key to Our Survival

The importance of pursuing Jewish studies, *talmud Torah,* throughout our lives can be understood through the legend of Rabbi Akiva, who lived in the Land of Israel when the Romans ruled. Although the Romans forbade the study of Torah, Rabbi Akiva continued his studies. When asked why he was willing to risk his life for the sake of studying Torah, Rabbi Akiva explained, "Just as fish need water to live, so the Jewish people need Torah. Though it may be dangerous to continue studying, it would be far more dangerous to stop." And with that, the rabbi smiled and returned to his study of Torah.

WHAT IMPACT DO YOU THINK ENDING YOUR JEWISH EDUCATION AS A TEEN WOULD HAVE ON YOUR ABILITY TO REACH YOUR FULL POTENTIAL AS AN ADULT? WHY? WHAT IMPACT DO YOU THINK IT COULD HAVE ON THE JEWISH COMMUNITY? WHY?

THE GREATEST MITZVAH

Two Talmudic sages, Rabbi Tarfon and Rabbi Akiva, struggled to determine which is more important—the study of Torah or living according to its laws. Rabbi Tarfon was convinced that it is more important to follow the laws of Torah. Rabbi Akiva argued that the only way to know what the laws are is to study Torah.

In the end, the sages determined that the study of Torah is greater than all other mitzvot because it leads to them all.

Rabbi Louis Finkelstein said: "When I pray, I talk to God. When I study, God talks to me." To end our studies is to cut short such conversations. In other words, without the benefit of *talmud Torah* we are less able to hear God, to struggle with our doubts and to expand and mature our beliefs, to fulfill the Covenant, and to pass on our tradition to the next generation.

Keeping informed about Israeli politics and culture through books, newspapers, lectures, and the Internet can help you find ways to express your love of Israel: Is tzedakah needed? Should you participate in a peace rally? Is there an Israeli movie or art exhibit that you can attend? How about a trip to Israel that includes studying Hebrew at an ulpan or volunteering at an archaeological dig?

Reading folktales about long-ago European, Chinese, Indian, and North African Jewish communities that cared for travelers and the poor may help you hear God's small, still voice inside your soul. It may remind you to reach out to friends and strangers by inviting them for Shabbat or holiday dinners, and to the needy through clothing or food drives.

It's a Dilemma!

YOU WANT TO CONTINUE YOUR JEWISH EDUCATION BUT YOUR HEBREW HIGH SCHOOL MEETS ON THE SAME DAY AS BASKETBALL PRACTICE. YOU ENJOY SPORTS AND HOPE SOMEDAY TO MAKE THE VARSITY TEAM. CAN YOU AVOID MAKING AN ALL-OR-NOTHING CHOICE? WHY?

_____

_____

WHAT DO YOU CONSIDER THE BEST PRACTICAL SOLUTION TO THIS DILEMMA? WHY?

_____

_____

_____

_____

Visiting chat rooms in which the weekly *parashah,* or Torah portion, is discussed can deepen your understanding of why Jews are obligated to pursue peace, care for our bodies, honor our parents, and observe Shabbat. As you mature, not only can continuing your studies deepen your understanding, it also can help you find new ways to fulfill these mitzvot.

We Study Torah as a Community

Our sages teach that we all stood at Mount Sinai; every Jewish soul that ever was and ever will be was present to hear God's voice and to accept its share in the Covenant. Just as God revealed the Torah as we stood together, so we are encouraged to study our sacred texts in community. When we study together—rabbis, teachers, students, and families in synagogues, schools, and homes—it is as if we are helping one another remember what we heard long ago at Sinai.

When we study in community with others, we can contribute our ideas to the group and learn from the wisdom of others. We can struggle together as Rabbi Tarfon and Rabbi Akiva did, arriving at new understandings of sacred texts. The more we learn, the more we have to give; and the stronger we become as individuals and as a community.

◀ **By continuing your studies you not only help ensure that our tradition will survive but also that it will continue to be enriched.**

SPEAKING OF THE TORAH, THE TALMUDIC SAGE BEN BAG BAG SAID, "TURN IT AGAIN AND AGAIN, FOR EVERYTHING IS IN IT; THINK ABOUT IT, GROW GRAY AND OLD OVER IT, AND DO NOT STRAY FROM IT, FOR THERE IS NO GREATER GOOD."

WHAT DO YOU THINK BEN BAG BAG MEANS? HOW CAN YOU APPLY THIS STATEMENT TO YOUR LIFE?

_____

_____

_____

_____

Show Respect For Sacred Books

Ever since Muhammad, Jews have been known as the "People of the Book" because of our special relationship to the book of books, the Torah. While other ancient peoples worshipped by sacrificing people or animals, Jews developed a form of worship that centered on reading as a sacred act. To this day, Shabbat services include the practice of carrying a book (the Torah scroll) around the sanctuary while the congregants reach out to touch and kiss it. Below are three additional ways to show respect for our sacred books.

- *Never place a sacred book on the ground.* Instead, put the book on a chair or a table, or hold it in your lap.
- *Never use a sacred book as a mat for some other object.* In other words, don't put a soda can on top of the Bible!
- *Should a sacred book fall on the ground by accident, kiss the book after retrieving it.* This traditional response affirms that the dropping of the book was not a display of contempt. It also affirms the preciousness of the book's contents.

Self-Portrait

★ **I like to spend my free time:** (Check as many responses as are appropriate)

_____ GOING TO MOVIES

_____ HANGING OUT WITH FRIENDS

_____ PLAYING COMPETITIVE SPORTS

_____ READING

_____ LISTENING TO MUSIC

_____ WATCHING SPECTATOR SPORTS

_____ ON-LINE

_____ WATCHING TV

_____ WORKING OUT

_____ WRITING

_____ PLAYING VIDEO GAMES

_____ PLAYING BOARD GAMES

_____ PAINTING OR DRAWING

_____ WITH MY FAMILY

_____ GOING TO PARTIES

Other: _____

_____

★ My favorite book is _____

★ My favorite radio station is _____

★ My favorite Web site is _____

★ **I would enjoy spending time with other Jewish teens who want to:** (Check as many responses as are appropriate)

_____ VISIT A JEWISH MUSEUM

_____ SEE AN ISRAELI MOVIE

_____ DO VOLUNTEER WORK

_____ LEAD A JUNIOR CONGREGATION

_____ EXPLORE JEWISH WEB SITES

_____ GO ISRAELI FOLK DANCING

_____ DISCUSS JEWISH ISSUES

_____ OBSERVE SHABBAT

_____ WORK ON A TZEDAKAH PROJECT

Other: _____

_____

_____

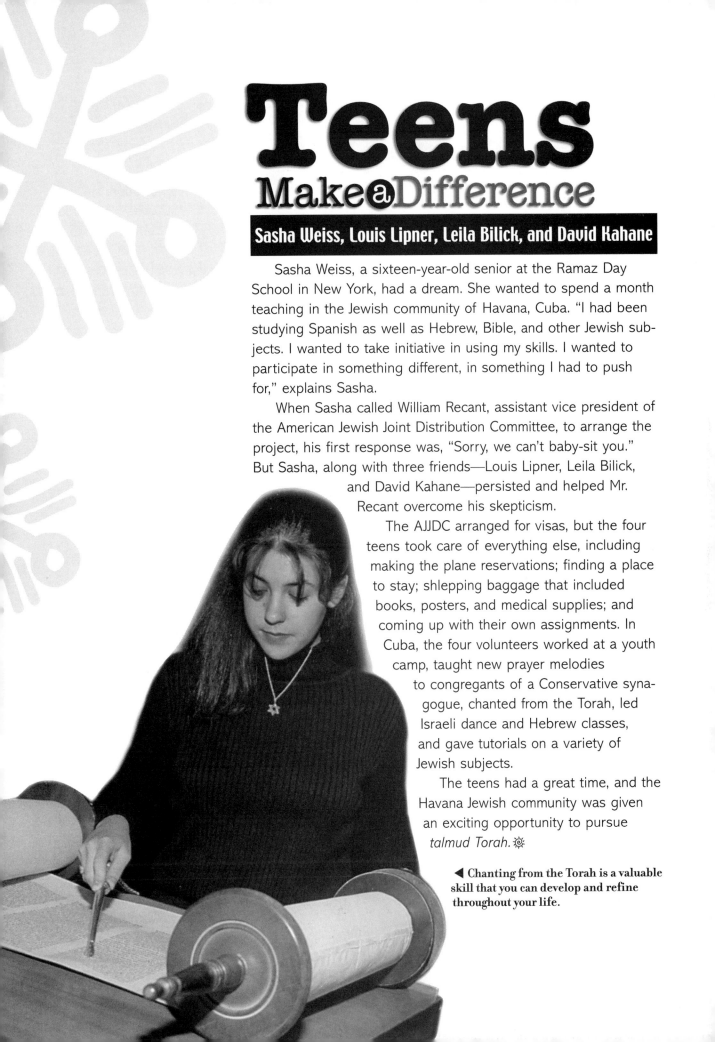

Teens
Make a Difference

Sasha Weiss, Louis Lipner, Leila Bilick, and David Kahane

Sasha Weiss, a sixteen-year-old senior at the Ramaz Day School in New York, had a dream. She wanted to spend a month teaching in the Jewish community of Havana, Cuba. "I had been studying Spanish as well as Hebrew, Bible, and other Jewish subjects. I wanted to take initiative in using my skills. I wanted to participate in something different, in something I had to push for," explains Sasha.

When Sasha called William Recant, assistant vice president of the American Jewish Joint Distribution Committee, to arrange the project, his first response was, "Sorry, we can't baby-sit you." But Sasha, along with three friends—Louis Lipner, Leila Bilick, and David Kahane—persisted and helped Mr. Recant overcome his skepticism.

The AJJDC arranged for visas, but the four teens took care of everything else, including making the plane reservations; finding a place to stay; shlepping baggage that included books, posters, and medical supplies; and coming up with their own assignments. In Cuba, the four volunteers worked at a youth camp, taught new prayer melodies to congregants of a Conservative synagogue, chanted from the Torah, led Israeli dance and Hebrew classes, and gave tutorials on a variety of Jewish subjects.

The teens had a great time, and the Havana Jewish community was given an exciting opportunity to pursue *talmud Torah*. ☀

◀ Chanting from the Torah is a valuable skill that you can develop and refine throughout your life.

The survival of Judaism is dependent on the willingness of all Jews, not just rabbis and scholars, to pursue the study of Torah throughout their lives. Here are some ideas for how you can continue to pursue *talmud Torah* beyond your current studies.

Ready! Set! GO!

 **Read the Ten Commandments.** In antiquity, the Ten Commandments were part of the morning prayer service (in both the Temple and the ancient synagogues). Although no longer read as part of the synagogue service, the private contemplation of the Ten Commandments has always been encouraged, no less now than in the past. (The Ten Commandments are found in *Exodus 20:2–14*.) Start by reading the commandments once a week or once a month, then try to increase the frequency until reading them is part of your daily routine.

 **Continue to study Hebrew.** French may be the language of love, but Hebrew is the language of holiness—the language of our sacred texts, our prayers, and the Land of Israel. It is also the language that connects Jews around the world and throughout the generations. The more Hebrew you know, the more fully you can participate in Jewish life.

Read books on Jewish subjects. Thousands of books—fiction and nonfiction—are available, on every conceivable subject, from Jewish sports heroes to Jewish history. There are books on Israeli art, Yiddish songs and humor, holidays, kosher cooking, commentary on biblical texts, and novels about the American-Jewish experience. These books can provide entertainment as well as insight into our tradition and an advanced Jewish education.

▲ Confirmation students can continue their Jewish education throughout high school and college. Just as we reread the Torah year after year in synagogue, so our tradition teaches us to continue our Jewish studies throughout our lives.

5 **Teach others.** The best way to learn is to teach. For example, volunteer to be a teacher's aide in your religious school or to teach Hebrew in a nursing home. The ultimate act of *talmud Torah* is one in which you share the joy of learning with someone else. By doing so, you build a stronger community.

▼ Filled with fun and interesting activities, such as water and team sports, Judaic arts and crafts, conversational Hebrew, and discussions of Jewish history, tradition, and culture, Jewish summer camps leave little time for cleaning your bunk...

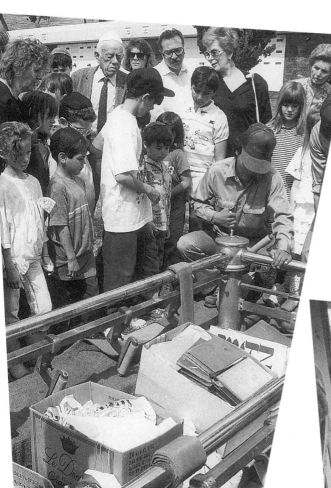

▲ Jewish law prohibits us from destroying anything with God's name on it. Rather, we place worn or damaged ritual objects, such as prayer shawls and tefillin as well as prayer books and Bibles, in a storage room called a genizah, or we bury them in a cemetery with the same care and dignity given to a person who has died. This burial of sacred books and objects was held in a Jewish cemetery in Los Angeles.

4 **Spend your free time with other teens who want to be Jewishly involved.** By joining a Junior Congregation or a Jewish youth movement, such as United Synagogue Youth (USY), North American Federation of Temple Youth (NFTY), or Young Judaea, and by attending a Jewish summer camp, such as Kutz Camp, Ramah, or Tel Yehudah, you will not only have a great time and develop terrific friendships, you will also become a more knowledgeable Jew.

To deepen my commitment to the mitzvah of *talmud Torah*, I chose to _____

_____

because _____

_____

This is what I did (provide a detailed description): _____

_____

_____

_____

I would/wouldn't choose to do this again because _____

_____

What I learned about myself by performing this mitzvah is _____

_____

Continuing my Jewish education is of great/moderate/little importance to me because

_____

_____

My other thoughts on observing this mitzvah: _____

_____

_____

_____

_____

_____

_____

15 Going Forward

Blessed are You, Adonai our God, Ruler of the universe, who makes us holy through Your mitzvot...

Each time we recite the blessing over Shabbat or holiday candles or the *b'rachah* for dwelling in a sukkah, read the scroll of Esther, welcome a child into our Covenant with God, affix a mezuzah to a doorpost, or put on a tallit, we are reminded that the mitzvot—the sacred actions we take—are our connection to God, our lifeline to holiness, Jewish tradition, and community. We are also reminded that the opportunity to become our best selves and to add holiness to the world through the mitzvot presents itself many times and in many ways on any given day.

This opportunity is present when we care for our bodies and for the world around us, when we eat and when we share our food, when we pursue peace and when we seek justice, when we choose to speak and when we choose to be silent. It is present from the time we rise up to the time we go to bed; on holy days and ordinary days; at home and in synagogue; in hospitals, parks, playgrounds, food banks, classrooms, hockey fields, concert halls, and anywhere else we find ourselves.

Let There Be Light!

Just as God brought light into the world on the first day of Creation, so it is our task to live as partners with God, continually adding light by performing the mitzvot. We can succeed by ever deepening our knowledge of Jewish tradition and broadening the scope of our observance, one mitzvah at a time. We can strengthen our resolve by studying and working together as a community and by living with an awareness of God's presence in our lives.

May your life be long, and may the light you add be bright and everlasting. May each mitzvah you fulfill contribute to the glory of God's name and the holiness of the Jewish people.

Lech l'cha, lechi lach. "Go forward," for you shall be a blessing and you shall be blessed.

Resources

American Cancer Society
1599 Clifton Road NE
Atlanta, GA 30329
800-227-2345
Web site: www.cancer.org

American Friends of the
Red Magen David Adom
888 Seventh Avenue, Suite 503
New York, NY 10106
E-mail: armdi@att.net

Bank Hapoalim
1177 Avenue of the Americas, 11th Floor
New York, NY 10036
212-782-2000
Web site: bankhapoalim.co.il

Bank Leumi
579 Fifth Avenue
New York, NY 10017
917-542-2343
Web site: www.bankleumiusa.com
E-mail: askus@bankleumi.co.il

Coalition on the Environment and
Jewish Life (COEJL)
443 Park Avenue South
New York, NY 10011
212-684-6950
Web site: www.coejl.org
E-mail: webmaster@coejl.org

Israel Ministry of Tourism
800 Second Avenue
New York, NY 10017
212-499-5660, 888-77-ISRAEL
Web site: www.goisrael.com
E-mail: info@goisrael.com

Jerusalem Post
270 Lafayette Street, Suite 505
New York, NY 10012
212-226-0955
Web site: www.jpost.com
E-mail: usoffice@jpost.co.il

Jerusalem Report
270 Lafayette Street, Suite 505
New York, NY 10012
212-226-8107
Web site: www.jrep.com
E-mail: usoffice@jpost.co.il

Jewish National Fund (JNF)
42 East 69th Street
New York, NY 10021
212-879-9300
Web site: www.jnf.org

Mazon: The Jewish Response to Hunger
12401 Wilshire Boulevard, Suite 303
Los Angeles, CA 90025
310-442-0020
Web site: www.mazon.org
E-mail: mazonmail@aol.com

Mizrachi Bank
611 Wilshire Boulevard
Los Angeles, CA 90017
213-362-2999

New Israel Fund
1101 14th Street NW
Washington, DC 20005
202-842-0900
Web site: www.nif.org
E-mail: info@nif.org

North American Federation of
Temple Youth (NFTY)
633 Third Avenue, 7th Floor
New York, NY 11017
212-650-4070
Web site: www.nfty.org
E-mail: nfty@nfty.org

Operation Sports Stuff
c/o Mark Guterman
1 Sheridan Drive
Short Hills, NJ 07078
973-379-4387

Red Cross
430 17th Street NW
Washington, DC 20006
202-737-8300
Web site: www.redcross.org
E-mail: internet@usa.redcross.org

State of Israel Bonds
575 Lexington Avenue, 6th Floor
New York, NY 10022
212-644-2663, 800-229-9650
Web site: www.israelbonds.com
E-mail: webmaster@israelbonds.com

20/20 Vision
1828 Jefferson Place NW
Washington, DC 20036
800-669-1782
Web site: www.2020vision.org
E-mail: vision@2020vision.org

United Jewish Appeal (UJA)
130 East 59th Street
New York, NY 10022
212-980-1000
Web site: www.ujafedny.org
E-mail: contact@ujafedny.org

Young Judaea
50 West 58th Street
New York, NY 10019
212-303-8014
Web site: www.youngjudaea.org
E-mail: info@youngjudaea.org

Ziv Tzedakah Fund
384 Wyoming Avenue
Millburn, NJ 07041
973-763-9396
Web site: www.ziv.org
E-mail: zivtzedaka@aol.com

Use this space to keep a record of additional resources you locate.